WELL READ,
WELL FED

Dedication

For Michelle Lewis and Anita Clearfield,
my partners in crime and poetry.

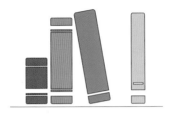

Published by Sellers Publishing, Inc.

Text © 2015 Marcia F. Brown
Layout & Design © Sellers Publishing, Inc.
Cover Illustration © 2015 Ashley Halsey, www.ashleyphalsey.com
All rights reserved.

Sellers Publishing, Inc.
161 John Roberts Road, South Portland, Maine 04106
Visit our Web site: www.sellerspublishing.com • E-mail: rsp@rsvp.com

ISBN 13: 978-1-4162-4564-3
Library of Congress Control Number: 2015930719

10 9 8 7 6 5 4 3 2 1

Printed and bound in China.

WELL READ, WELL FED

A YEAR OF GREAT READS AND SIMPLE DISHES FOR BOOK GROUPS

With best wishes,

Marcia Brown

MARCIA F. BROWN

October 2015

SELLERS
PUBLISHING

contents

introduction

Any reader or writer who has ever been part of a regular monthly book group or writing workshop for a period of time knows that what starts out as a setting for literary gravitas sustained by bottled water and a bowl of pretzels soon evolves into a feast for mind and body, with an increasing emphasis on the body. Where like-minded friends and former English majors initially commit to reading one worthwhile tome a month, then sitting down to share their insights on the work, these convivial gatherings — away from job, family, and chores for a few hours — inevitably become half informal dinner party, half bookish discussion. This is as it should be.

The pleasures of the mind are always enhanced by the comfort of the body. In *A Room of One's Own*, Virginia Woolf famously observed, "One cannot think well, love well, sleep well, if one has not dined well." *Well Read, Well Fed* is an endorsement of these deliciously stolen hours, when women (and some men — kudos to them, as statistically, American book groups are overwhelmingly formed and attended by women) spend an evening together, catching up on news, friendships, family, and yes, politics, entertainment, health, fashion, gripes, and gossip, over a glass of wine and light food — and *then*, the stimulation of discussing a good book shared. Every group differs in its specific format, but the basics are akin. Some book groups meet in local restaurants, bars, coffee shops, or community rooms, but I have chosen to write about groups that meet in the homes of the participants, where light refreshments are put forth, conversation is wide ranging, and the reading and writing of literature is *eventually* discussed.

I belong to a poetry writing workshop. I have many friends in book groups and know one wonderful local club of older couples who meet monthly to share a meal and read poems aloud to one another — and not one member is an avowed poet or writer. They simply read and enjoy poetry together, which I find wondrous. Whatever the format or focus, it is evident that many busy people find their book group or workshop evening a rich and enjoyable respite, and we ought to celebrate this wonderful phenomenon of humanism as a bright spot in our cultural evolution. *Well Read, Well Fed* serves up a sampling of suggested reading and simple but thoughtful food preparations that I hope will provide book lovers, readers, and home cooks with some ideas and enthusiastic encouragement to carry on this happy tradition.

Marcia F. Brown
March 2015

book notes

The books I suggest to readers herein — novels, short-story collections, nonfiction, plays, essays, and poetry — are not chosen as literary *tours de force* (though some surely are), or to suggest any sort of updated canon, but for sheer readability and pleasure. I have read almost all of them myself. Some are classics that simply speak for themselves, and some come highly recommended by readers I trust. I have been referring these and other favorites to friends long before I thought of writing this book. As of this writing, all are in print and readily available at bookstores and libraries or online. Many will lend themselves to good, lively discussion for book groups, but perhaps not all. You can find lists of book club recommendations at any number of Web sites or in bookstores, or identify them readily by the author Q&A or book club notes at the end of new paperback editions. Many of the "good reads" I suggest here simply offer the delights of fine literature: sublime writing, a seductive narrative, or wit and wisdom passed down through the ages. These pleasures are good to share among friends.

And one more note: If you are reading this book, you are doubtless a book lover and therefore, I hope, a *bookstore* lover. If your group chooses to read one of the many books I suggest herein, I hope you will buy your copies from your local bookstore. This support is enormously important. If you believe, as I do, that local, independent bookstores are the heart and soul of reading communities, shared discoveries in literature, and the celebration of books themselves, then give them your patronage.

recipe notes

My workshops have all had at least one vegetarian member, and these days, it seems we are all questioning the right amount, if any, of meat we should consume. And because these are light meals before a largely sedentary evening, the menus do not include red meat or poultry and are vegetable or seafood based. You can always add or substitute meats if your group prefers. Because we often meet on weeknights after work, the 12 main dishes here are intended to be healthful and simple to prepare. They may be made a day ahead or, in some cases, further in advance and frozen if the host or hostess is pressed for time. I have sized the recipes for four to five medium portions, but all can be easily reduced or increased. We usually have wine (though drivers may want coffee or tea) and a few nuts or other snacks on hand. We share a light supper and perhaps set out a plate of sliced fruit, cookies, or sweets for later in the evening.

We know each other well, and we understand that hosting the book club should not be a stressful event. All of us have been known to order out pizzas or relocate to the local diner when the kitchen faucet suddenly fails or it's been an impossible day at the office. The menus here are offered for those who have a little time to prepare and are looking for a ready idea for a good meal to serve a small group. The recipes have been enjoyed by my workshop members, and some originated in their kitchens. I have happily added them to my own repertoire. Add, alter, embellish, and personalize the dishes to your own tastes — that's what being part of a creative community is all about.

JANUARY / WARM READS

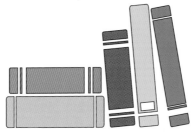

One must have a mind of winter . . . and
have been cold a long time . . .

–Wallace Stevens, "The Snow Man"

A GOOD READER, like a true romantic, knows that surrender is the key to falling in love. Once we suspend analytic instincts and simply move into the story, we have become a book lover. Yet from our first book report in elementary school through college or graduate studies, we are rarely allowed this luxury.

When I was young and trying to earn a living in New York City, I worked for several years as a professional reader for film studios. Paid by the "property" — i.e., book, screenplay, or, most often, enormous photocopied manuscript (these were the days before home computers, e-mail, or downloads) — I speed-read and wrote "coverage" on dozens of books a week to pay my rent. Since our rate of pay as readers was based on page length, we all grabbed for the back-breakers. The manuscript for Helen Hooven Santmyer's ". . . And Ladies of the Club" weighed in at an astonishing 2,500-plus pages, to be dispatched in a weekend. Likewise Allan Gurganus's Oldest Living Confederate Widow Tells All. Somewhere after page 1,000, I willed the widow to just expire. With a pad and pen at my side, noting characters' names and plot turns, I had no time to actually enjoy the books — I just inhaled them and ran to my work station to type up (yes, on a typewriter) my reader's synopsis, along with my invoice, so I could get paid before the landlord came calling. I have no idea who, if anyone, read most of these reports. But I do know that when I finally left the city and that line of work, it took me years to relearn the simple joy of reading a good book.

To launch my reacquaintance with so-called (I had my doubts) "pleasure reading," I picked up John Irving's *The Cider House Rules*, since I had adored his *The World According to Garp* and *The Hotel New Hampshire*. But for whatever reasons, some of the graphic medical descriptions made me weak and queasy. I put it down. Just like that. This was a whole new freedom, I realized: the right not to finish a book. I felt liberated. Of course, I am sorry it happened to be that novel, because I later saw the movie and went back and did read the whole book and enjoyed it, so another lesson learned: sometimes books appeal or fail to, depending on where you are in your life. It's okay to put them down unfinished. It's okay to pick them up again when your outlook changes. The important thing is to keep reaching for those most miraculous of human communications we call books — those odd little markings on paper (stone tablets, papyrus, or cyberspace) by men and women we'll likely never meet, but who tell us wondrous stories about their worlds, real and imagined. Books — along with music and art — are as close as we come to immortality. However you get them, don't ever give up on books. And I say this as a recovering professional reader.

Because I am an orderly person, and because I determined that this book would follow a calendar year, I am starting here with January

— the month when it is simply too miserable in most of the Northern Hemisphere to venture out for book groups or much of anything except showing up at your job or buying essential food and drink. When I was growing up in Massachusetts, my father was constantly tuned in to winter radio bulletins of incoming weather, which he treated as personal, top-brass mission from the weather gods that sent him charging out to the stores for emergency provisions and "supplies." For reasons unknown to us, these items usually consisted of dozens of cans of creamed corn and stewed tomatoes that we all hated, along with packs of candles, though we always had plenty on hand from previous storm threats that failed to materialize. I don't remember using any of it. Ever.

In Maine, where I live, blizzards, ice storms, power outages, and what my friend, poet Baron Wormser, calls the plain "blunt misery of January" conspire to keep us home. We are forever canceling and rescheduling gatherings of all sorts, including book club meetings. (That's a good thing if you haven't found time to read your monthly book pick.) In any case, there are few occasions more conducive to reading than a bona fide snow day. For those of us who are not zealous winter-sports enthusiasts, one of winter's saving graces is the luxury of wrapping up on the couch for an afternoon with a good book.

january reads

Here, for January readers, are some wonderful fireside tales and poetry collections with warm-climate settings that should hearten even the most snowbound reader. If you do get a clear stretch of weather and can hold your book group gathering, I promise that everyone will be grateful to reflect on these temperate sceneries and not Lord Shackleton's expedition on the *Endurance*.

Joe Bolton, *The Last Nostalgia: Poems 1982–1990*, edited by Donald Justice
A posthumously compiled collection by one of the most compelling young voices in American poetry, tragically silenced by suicide at age 28 in 1990. These transcendently beautiful poems, set in Florida, Arizona, and Bolton's home state of Kentucky, make us grateful for his early talents and also lament his loss and the absence of mature work.

Gerald Durrell, *My Family and Other Animals*
English author Gerald Durrell's delightful account of his family's time spent living on the Greek island of Corfu when he was ten years old. A charmer for readers of all ages.

Dave Eggers, *A Hologram for the King*
A comic parable of America in the global economy, from one of our most perceptive observers. Sent to an unnamed Middle Eastern kingdom to make a sales pitch to its king, Eggers's protagonist is an Everyman for the modern business age in this deft and surprisingly tender novel.

John Fowles, *The Magus*
A young Englishman accepts a teaching assignment on a remote Greek island where fantasy and reality challenge the young teacher's sanity. By the master storyteller and author of *The French Lieutenant's Woman*.

Carl Hiaasen, *Double Whammy*

The first in Hiaasen's series of hilarious, addictive comic novels featuring the unlikely hero and neophyte private eye R. J. Decker, and introducing the ex-governor-turned-hermit-philosopher Skink. A bizarre cast of characters populates this outrageous comedy, where people keep getting killed at a Florida bass fishing tournament. *Double Whammy* launched and justifies Hiaasen's runaway reputation as a great American comic novelist.

Shara McCallum, *This Strange Land*

Jamaican-born poet Shara McCallum probes the meaning of motherland, history, personal diaspora, identity, and memory in these beautifully crafted, musical poems.

Carson McCullers, *The Member of the Wedding*

The novel that became an award-winning play and major motion picture. Twelve-year-old Frankie becomes enamored with the romantic notion of her brother's upcoming wedding and fashions for herself an outsize role in the proceedings. McCullers's delicately wrought masterpiece shades the pain of adolescence with uncommon compassion.

Toni Morrison, *Song of Solomon*

Pulitzer Prize–winning author Toni Morrison's 1977 masterpiece, chronicling four generations of unforgettable characters in a black family — mistakenly surnamed Dead, due to an error in the roster of slaves — beginning with Macon (nicknamed "Milkman") Dead III. This is a powerful, lyrical, and thoroughly absorbing novel by one of America's greatest storytellers.

Pablo Neruda, *Isla Negra: A Notebook [poems]*

From his house on the shores of his beloved Isla Negra, Neruda meditates on the ocean as a living metaphor for the dazzling natural world around him. A gorgeous work by the man considered by many to be the greatest poet writing in any language in the 20th century.

Ann Patchett, *State of Wonder*

A pharmaceutical researcher sets off into the Amazon jungle to recover the remains and personal effects of a colleague who mysteriously died while working there. The plot is as riveting and unpredictable as its jungle setting. Patchett has us blindly and thrillingly following her deeper and deeper into this surreal and absorbing tale.

Arundhati Roy, *The God of Small Things*

A lush narrative of a wealthy Indian family and its pair of young twins — so inextricably connected that they fall asleep and share the same little dreams — and what transpires when their world is disrupted by a young cousin's arrival. Roy's quietly elegant prose captivates in this acclaimed novel.

Karen Russell, *Swamplandia!*

The story of 12-year-old Ava Bigtree, an alligator wrestler in her family's run-down Florida Everglades theme park. When her mother falls ill and the family is plunged into chaos, Ava sets off through the swamplands on an odyssey to recover her runaway sister.

Wallace Stegner, *Angle of Repose*

Stegner's Pulitzer Prize–winning novel of retired American historian Lyman Ward, who sets out to research and write about his remarkable grandparents' exploration of the Western frontier, and makes unexpected discoveries about his own life in the process.

Derek Walcott, *Selected Poems*

Luminous, rich poems of the Caribbean from the prolific native St. Lucian poet. Winner of the Nobel Prize for Literature in 1992, Walcott is a unique modern poet who weaves traditional island influences and patois with contemporary cultural perspectives.

on the menu

MEDITERRANEAN LENTIL SOUP

In all your life you will be hard-pressed to find
something as simple, soothing, and forgiving,
as consoling as lentil soup.

–Laurie Colwin, *More Home Cooking*

I agree with the wonderful novelist and food writer Laurie Colwin, who was stolen from us when she was far too young and at the height of her considerable talents. I treasure my faded and dog-eared copies of her *Home Cooking* and *More Home Cooking* — in fact, food-enthusiastic book groups could do worse than to include these on their reading list, as well as her delightful novels. She wrote for *Gourmet* magazine for several years in an engaging, flippant style that debunked myths of perfection in holiday cooking or entertaining anyone, or just feeding a hungry family day in and day out. I miss her, and I never met her. She's that kind of writer.

In some other life, I'm sure I was Mediterranean. The Mediterranean diet has become much touted in recent years for its reliance on vegetables, grains, and other elements generally considered low on the food chain. Historically, this diet has had more to do with terrain and economics than health or social consciousness. If you've ever stayed in a remote mountain village, you know you don't just run to the store for some hamburger. You keep rice and beans and flour at home, and you grow or shop locally for fruits and vegetables that must be stored and preserved for as long as possible. Meat and fish, unless you raise or catch it, are expensive and hard to keep in hot climates, and so are used sparingly to enrich grain and vegetable dishes and for special occasions. Olive oil is your most important kitchen staple. This diet, born of necessity, turns out to be one of the best things you can do for your health.

When I was first out of college and broker than broke, I made lentil soup for my guests — it is amazingly filling, good for you, requires only one kettle large enough to hold a lot of soup, and costs almost nothing to make. It likes to be served in nice earthenware crocks or bowls, but if you are young and your table-settings department is still a bit sketchy, you can always serve it in big coffee mugs if you don't have enough bowls to go around. Add a dollop of Greek-style yogurt and garnish it with fresh dill if you are feeling fancy, but it really stands up quite well as is.

This is not Laurie Colwin's recipe for lentil soup, but it is a good one, easy to make ahead and bursting with vitamins, fiber, and other things readers need to get them through the short days of a long winter. I feel certain she would approve. This is more or less the version that was taught to me by my Greek American friend. She once delivered a medicinal quart container of it to my New York apartment, where I lay languishing from some miserable winter flu, and to this day I credit it with curing me overnight. If you feel some malady coming on, I cannot think of a better way to head it off than with a large bowl of this good lentil soup served very hot. And don't omit the vinegar — I think it may be the magic ingredient.

• MEDITERRANEAN LENTIL SOUP •

2 tbsp. olive oil
1 large clove garlic, minced
1 medium onion, finely diced
2 large carrots, diced
2 stalks celery, diced
4 cups beef or vegetable stock*
3 cups water
1 large (28 oz) can of crushed tomatoes
2 cups green or red lentils, rinsed and checked over for stones
2 bay leaves
Sea salt
1–2 tbsp. good red wine vinegar
Freshly ground pepper

Optional: Plain or Greek yogurt and fresh dill, for serving

*I favor beef stock for lentil soup, but if your guests are vegetarian,
*   vegetable stock may be substituted.*

Serves 6

Preparation: In a large, deep kettle, heat olive oil over medium-high heat. Add garlic and onion and sauté until onion is soft, about 4–5 minutes. Stir in chopped carrots and celery and cook until slightly softened, about 5 minutes. Add stock, water, tomatoes, rinsed lentils, bay leaves, and a good pinch of sea salt. Bring to boil and simmer 1 hour, or until lentils are softened. Add the vinegar, and salt and pepper to taste. This may be made a day or two in advance and chilled, though the soup will tend to thicken, so you may want to add a bit more liquid when reheating over a low burner. Serve in large soup bowls, with a generous dollop of plain or Greek yogurt and a sprinkle of fresh dill.

This soup is substantial and constitutes a balanced meal by itself. If you want to expand the meal a little, serve it with a simple green salad, lightly dressed with lemon juice and olive oil, and a rustic bread. In January it is easy to find nice tangerines and those bags of little clementines — you might put out a plate of peeled and sliced citrus sections, along with almond or anisette cookies to enjoy after the meal.

FEBRUARY / LOVE STORIES

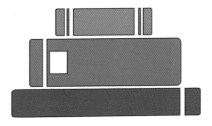

At the touch of love, everyone becomes a poet.

–Plato

FEBRUARY'S BLUE COLD and icy moons would make us grateful it's a short month, but for that sweet, lace-trimmed, sentimental holiday smack in its middle. My husband and I make a point to celebrate it. This is largely my doing, I admit, but we always find valentine cards from each other on the breakfast table, and I usually try to make him something festive to eat: sliced strawberries with scones, or cranberry bread in a heart-shaped pan. One February 14th, back when we kept horses, I received from my husband a bright red manure fork, into the handle of which he had lovingly wood-burned my initials. It is by far my favorite valentine ever.

February does give your book group a great excuse to read or reread some of literature's enduring love stories. What makes a great romance on the page is a bit elusive. Sometimes it can be the same thing that works in the movies: ill-matched, star-crossed, socially unacceptable, or forbidden lovers seeming to exhaust every effort of free will to resist each other, or to overcome mountainous obstacles placed in their path by others. They might land in each other's arms in the end or not — like Meryl Streep's Isak Dinesen and Robert Redford's Denys Finch Hatton in *Out of Africa*, compounding the heartache. Sometimes it is characters who are quirky and ill-matched, but when thrown together by circumstances, discover the best in each other — think of Bogart and Hepburn in *The African Queen*. Love stories, thwarted or ending happily ever after, have pleased and entertained readers mightily for centuries and presumably will continue to do so.

There is a growing body of wonderful young adult (YA) fiction that explores the tender stirrings of first love — its sweetness as well as its agonizing disappointments. Many of these books, like Marcus Zusak's extraordinary historical novel, *The Book Thief*, or *Ruby Red Heart in a Cold Blue Sea* by the talented Maine writer Morgan Callan Rogers, have attracted wide audiences beyond the conventional YA market. I also rank highly as mature love stories, John Bayley's autobiographical *Elegy for Iris* and Wendell Berry's beautiful novel *Hannah Coulter*. More complex than the classic love-conquers-all formula, these works introduce us to stories of abiding love, profound human devotion, and worthy characters whom we grow to admire and trust. They can give us, as readers, insight and inspiration to inform our own most important relationships.

In both the fiction and nonfiction worlds, there are eloquent stories of enduring love: the romance of two people who stay devotedly together through the ordinary, extraordinary ups and downs of a life. The stories can give us, as readers, insight and inspiration to inform our own most important relationships. And then there are just some crazy-quirky romantic inventions. One of my recent favorites is Eli Brown's 2013 novel, *Cinnamon and Gunpowder*, a love story cloaked in a 19th-century swashbuckling pirate adventure.

february reads

Whether your own Valentine's Day is divine or tends to fall flat, or your book group just feels the need to luxuriate in a romantic idyll, here are some tried-and-true heart-warmers to read for the first time or to revisit.

John Bayley, *Elegy for Iris*
> British writer John Bayley's tender account of his lifelong romance and 42-year marriage to renowned author Iris Murdoch, as Alzheimer's disease begins to take hold of her. Told with enormous delicacy, grace, and humor, this is a beautifully wrought love story of one of the great literary pairings of our time.

Wendell Berry, *Hannah Coulter*
> One of the most eloquent entries in Berry's multivolume Coulter family saga, set in Port William, Kentucky. This is a quiet, elegant, and wise novel of beautifully realized characters who, having survived the dislocations of World War II, must "live right on." Poet Berry's gorgeous prose lights up these pages.

Eli Brown, *Cinnamon and Gunpowder*
> Mad Hannah Mabbot, a ruthless and beautiful female pirate captain, kidnaps the prim chef of an English sea captain. The chef will be allowed to live as long as he can produce — from Mabbot's pathetic shipboard provisions — a sublime dinner for her once a week. Captive and captor, hunter and hunted, Hannah and her crew of devoted misfits race across oceans in pursuit of her nemesis in this unlikely and enchanting romp on the high seas, set against the backdrop of Great Britain's monopoly on the China trade routes and its fallout.

Michael Cunningham, *The Hours*
> Winner of the Pulitzer Prize, this poignant homage to Virginia Woolf's *Mrs. Dalloway* interweaves three intimate stories of

relationships — set respectively in 1923 London, Greenwich Village in the 1990s, and 1947 Los Angeles — into a seamless novel of struggle and redemption. Cunningham's beautifully nuanced prose gives us a great work of literature about great art.

Nicholas Evans, *The Horse Whisperer*
A best-selling novel, made into a Hollywood blockbuster directed by and starring Robert Redford. The original is a page-turner of familial strife and reconciliation, coming of age, and a troubled animal that can only be cured by a mystically gifted cowboy with talents both equine and human. Based on a real person, this "horse whispering" study is riveting.

Jack Finney, *Time and Again*
The beloved classic tale of time travel. Recruited by a secret government program, Si Morley mysteriously travels from his 1970s life in New York City to the City's bygone era of 1882. This addictive read is part sci-fi, part old-fashioned romance, and just pure escapist fun.

John Keats, *Letters of John Keats*
The young poet's timeless manifesto on the pursuit of Truth and Beauty in literature, revealed through his personal correspondence. Though he died of tuberculosis at age 25, Keats's short, impassioned life devoted to the poetic imagination still speaks to us across the ages.

Jerome Kilty, *Dear Liar*
A brilliantly witty two-person play based on the correspondence between George Bernard Shaw and Mrs. Patrick Campbell, the actress he adores but cannot have. The two are equally matched in this epistolary drama, a small gem both on the page and on the stage.

Nicole Krauss, *The History of Love*
Behind this opaque title is an astonishing book — both the literal subject of the story, which unfolds in multiple layers, and the hauntingly beautiful novel Krauss has created here. A modern must-read.

Ian McEwan, *Atonement*

The book that rightly put McEwan on the map, and a masterpiece of postmodern fiction. Set in 1935 in the English countryside, with a deception that lingers over decades and a World War, this is McEwan writing at his seamless best.

Margaret Mitchell, *Gone with the Wind*

The sweeping romantic saga of dueling passions in the Old South, set against the backdrop of the American Civil War. The novel contains some surprising historic insights, and it is well worth reading for those who have only seen the Hollywood extravaganza of Rhett Butler and his tempestuous Scarlett O'Hara.

Michael Ondaatje, *The English Patient*

Winner of the Booker Prize, Ondaatje's stunning and mysterious tale of four damaged souls sheltering in a desolate Italian monastery in the final days of World War II. Unlike any book you have read before, *The English Patient* is an utterly consuming memory poem that is impossible to forget.

Leo Tolstoy, *Anna Karenina* (Translated by Richard Pevear and Larissa Volokhonsky, Penguin Classics Edition)

The great Russian novel, whose concerns, themes, revelations, and tone remain surprisingly modern in this recent, pitch-perfect translation.

William Butler Yeats, *Collected Poems*

Poems of intellect, myth, and legend, of nature and rhapsody for his Irish homeland, and ardor for his beloved Maud Gonne. By one of the greatest poets of the English language.

on the menu

CHEESE FONDUE

Many's the long night I've dreamed of cheese
— toasted, mostly.

–Robert Louis Stevenson, *Treasure Island*

Pay no attention to that little voice in your head that says fondue went out with macramé and the orange enamel pot collecting dust in the garage. Not so. Fondue is alive and well, easy to make, satisfying in every way, and great fun for a group meal. It's always a change of pace, and even the most finicky gourmand will beam when a bubbling cheese fondue is set before him or her. I think it must be the way fondue signals *I am going to be gooey, hot, delicious, and not terribly serious . . . so relax and have fun.* There are even silly games played around the pot: for instance, tradition says that every dipper dropped in the pot presages one baby to be born to the fork holder.

I was served my first cheese fondue in Geneva, Switzerland, though that somehow seems almost too perfect. It is true. I was young and nervy, backpacking around Europe with two friends and no money, and had taken up a college friend on her offer to camp out in her Swiss boyfriend's dorm at the University of Geneva for a night or two. While this now strikes me as the setup for a harrowing made-for-TV crime show featuring a naïve young woman in peril, it blessedly turned out to be perfectly safe and great fun. Perhaps I had more sense back then than it now sounds like I did. In any case, my young host appeared at the train station to collect me — my two companions were to arrive later that evening — and announced that we would tour the city and then repair to his dorm suite for a fondue party with friends. And that is exactly what happened. As I recall, he went to some lengths setting up the fondue pot, heating up the rich winey-cheesy mixture, cutting bread, and putting out jugs of *vin ordinaire*. Gradually, the small room filled up with his fellow students and, eventually, my traveling companions. The fondue was delicious, and we all had a hilarious time exercising our schoolgirl French with the Swiss natives. I have had a soft spot for fondue ever since, and also for the wondrous dish called *raclette*, to which our university hosts also introduced us that night. Raclette is a semifirm Swiss cheese that gets heated on one side till it's all melty, then scraped off onto little boiled potatoes and served with pickles. I have no idea how they prepared it in the dormitory's little makeshift kitchenette, and I do not think I have had it since. You have to have the right raclette cheese. I have just given myself a craving for it with this writing and expect I will now have to go on a raclette cheese hunt.

In the first years of our relationship, my husband and I would often spend weekends going cross-country skiing with friends in the woods behind our house. After a good long ski, it became our custom to ski back to the house, tired, thirsty, and very hungry. We'd open a big bottle of wine and heat up some premade cheese fondue that we served in a rather grand old chafing dish. We ate it with chunks of toasted bread and a dish of roasted nuts and dried apricots, which someone always gave us for Christmas. Those were lovely winter afternoons with good friends. When our four grandsons came along, I discovered that few things made them happier at a big family gathering than my serving cheese fondue with cubes of toasted bread and chunks of vegetables for an hors d'oeuvre before dinner. Fondue makes it impossible for people to hold back the way they tend to do when you have a perfectly arranged platter of fancy canapés or forbidding wheels of uncut cheese and pâté. And growing boys can put away a startling amount of melted cheese and still enjoy dinner. While it might not work for your fanciest dinner party, cheese fondue to start out a casual gathering among familiars provides entertainment for all — I highly recommend it. It also makes a great cold-weather supper for book club night.

I will give you a basic recipe here, which is the kind I prefer. Some people like to add a bit of garlic, cayenne, nutmeg, or even a jolt of good tomato paste. That's gilding the lily to me. I will also tell you that there is an excellent premade Swiss fondue packet on the market that is perfectly acceptable if you are pressed for time. Just squeeze the foil envelope into the pot and heat it on the stove. A major discounted natural-foods chain also offers a very serviceable premade fondue, in about a pint-volume cardboard container that you can freeze for an indeterminate amount of time and heat up in the microwave when you want it. I still think "from scratch" is best, but whatever your preference, invest in a simple (cast iron is ideal) fondue pot, which will come with its own stand, sterno holder, and long-handled forks, and surprise yourself and your book club with how much fun fondue still is.

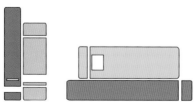

• BASIC CHEESE FONDUE •

1 tbsp. cornstarch

2 tsp. kirsch

1 1/2 cups white wine

1 lb. grated cheese, preferably a combination of Emmenthaler and
  Gruyère

Bread and/or fresh vegetables/fruits for dipping (see below)

Serves 6

Preparation: Whisk together cornstarch and kirsch and set aside. Heat wine in a fondue pot over medium-high heat on stove. When hot, slowly add grated cheese, stirring in swirling motions to blend. When cheese is melted and combined, add in kirsch mixture and heat until slightly thick. Carefully place the pot on fondue stand and light the sterno burner to serve.

For dipping: Tradition requires a good supply of high-quality bread cubes, such as sourdough, French baguette, whole wheat, multigrain, or any artisanal, crusty bread. Cut in cubes about 1" square. Toast slightly in a 300°F (150°C) oven to firm them up, if you like. If this is all you are dipping, serve the fondue with a mixed green salad, and you're set. However, there are also dozens of vegetables and fruits that make for great dipping. Some will need to be slightly blanched to soften them, such as broccoli and cauliflower florets, carrot chunks, winter squash, beets, kohlrabi, and new potatoes (halved). Others are fine to cut up raw: cherry tomatoes, snap peas, red and green peppers, radishes of all kinds, fennel bulbs (sliced), zucchini, summer squash, and apple and pear slices. Cooked shrimp or sausage pieces will also work well, if you're looking for more substance.

However you create your fondue, the people in your book club will love it. Set out small, individual plates for resting forks and catching drips — expect a lot of them — and serve with a robust red wine. A big plate of cinnamon wafers and chilled seedless grapes would make a nice chaser to enjoy with the book discussion.

MARCH / WANDERLUST

March comes in with an adder's head,
and goes out with a peacock's tail.

–Richard Lawson Gales

SOME YEARS AGO, my husband and I treated ourselves to a tour
of the northern Ionian Islands in Greece. We chartered a sailboat
for our first week of travel — I with some trepidation, since he is
the only sailor in the family, and I was pretty certain we ought to
have another hand on board, should anything go awry. As it turned
out, the seas and winds were gentle, my captain was more than
capable, and we spent an idyllic week sailing from one little island
to another, exploring harbors and villages.

We had arranged to spend a second week in a small, rented villa
on the northern coast of Corfu. While there was no discernable
reason ever to leave our villa, surrounded as it was by beach, sun,
climbing roses, and lemon trees, we loved taking daily trips out to
explore the surrounding countryside. Our transport was a blindingly
bright-green rental wagon of indeterminate make and model, and

our only guide a haphazard handful of tourist maps and childlike diagrams of the area, drawn by the local rental agent.

Corfu is one of the few abundantly verdant Greek islands. The northern coast boasts miles of ancient olive groves that in summer are crisscrossed with rolled black nets in anticipation of the harvest. We drove past rustic family farms with front yards full of well-fed pigs, wandering chickens, and big brown hares crouching in the dust. When we walked the little island roads, we'd peer through the gates of elegant pink and apricot villas, catching glimpses of hidden gardens, cool glazed tiles, and swimming pools. Each day was a sun-washed new adventure, and none was more memorable than the day we discovered Agios Stefanos.

We were not looking for it, but stumbled upon Agios Stefanos in that way of having taken the wrong turn from the main road, and once wrongheaded, deciding to pursue our wrongness to its conclusion. In this case, pursuit was straight down a mile-high cliff and almost headlong into the sea. On Corfu, as on most of the Greek islands, there is a certain fatalism in that moment when one of you says, "Let's just see where it goes." Straight ahead was a stretch of royal-blue sea and what appeared to be a little fishing village. We came upon a tiny parking lot for the beach area, where an old dog with a good face napped in the shade of a trailer. An aged man wearing a Greek sailor's cap was the lot's sole attendant. Obeying his vigorous arm signals, we maneuvered our rental between an olive tree and a dumpster. Serious as death about his parking lot, he slapped all sorts of stickers and flyers, permits and receipts onto the car, wedging them under the windshield wipers and into the crack of the door. Then, nodding approval, he withdrew back to his seat in the shade of a large tree.

That first visit to Agios Stefanos, we arrived just at lunchtime. We chose the busiest of the tavernas and wandered in under its grapevine canopy. It was cool under the vines and out of the hot sun, and we were early enough to choose a table by the water.

We asked our server to bring us some of the island's ubiquitous and good white wine that always arrived in an ice-cold aluminum pitcher — something like a lightweight German beer stein, and a fixture in the island tavernas.

We ordered salads that by now we knew would be small plates heaped with ripe garden tomatoes, sweet white onion, crisp slices of cucumber right out of the garden, salty feta, and brined olives, splashed with local olive oil and sprinkled with oregano. Then we simply sat back and basked in our good fortune: the sparkling day, the beautiful little bay and the mountains beyond, wine, the prospect of good food, and the one you love to share it with.

I count this trip among the most magical in my lifetime, filled as it was with this and other accidental discoveries of a perfect place. I travel back there in my mind when I need to remember how food that is sublime is often the most simple — and, as we have come to respect in recent years, consumed in its native *terroir*.

march reads

In New England where I live, we all need some sublimity in March. March can seem stuck. We just can't move on. It's not cold or warm, not green or white, just brown, gray, and muddy. The month seems to have at least 40 days in it. Our minds wander to foreign climes. I start surfing the travel Web sites for exotic locales I have no intention of visiting. I look up Italian villas for rent, Portuguese fishing villages, another Greek island charter. Lately I've been reading about trips up the Nile.

A palliative for this cyber wanderlust (and a far better use of one's time) is, of course, to curl up with one of the many wonderful travelogues, memoirs, and novels set in distant lands. Their authors have actually been there (as a rule), and good travel writers or novelists will share with you every hour of drenching sun, the cool damp of ancient castle walls, and the sounds of street musicians and bell-tower carillons. They can give you the scents, colors, and flavors of the marketplace — fragrant scoops of curry spices, the perfume of scotch broom and roadside field flowers, the restorative pleasure of a good local wine served with homemade pasta heaped with delicate mushrooms. And your trip is virtually all expense paid. Completely free, if you've got a library card. Here are some wonderful books for armchair traveling when you need to get far away. Or for just about any time.

Bill Bryson, *A Walk in the Woods: Rediscovering America on the Appalachian Trail*

> With his signature wit and appreciation for the absurd, travel writer Bill Bryson recounts hiking the Appalachian Trail, remarking upon the trail's history, ecology, natural wonders, and some rare characters — both two- and four-legged — that he encounters. One of Bryson's most popular books.

Louis De Bernieres, *Corelli's Mandolin*
Set against a hypnotic backdrop of ancient gods and fishermen
on the Greek island of Cephalonia. Pelagia, an aspiring healer
and headstrong beauty who is betrothed to a returning soldier,
must contend with questions of loyalty and betrayal as Italian
forces and the charismatic, mandolin-playing Captain Corelli set
up their garrison on the quiet island.

M. F. K. Fisher, *The Boss Dog*
Part memoir, part fiction, from the celebrated author and epicure.
A young mother's chronicle of her year in Aix-en-Provence with
her two precocious American daughters and a local mongrel who
frequents the cafés on the famed Cours Mirabeau.

Lily King, *Euphoria*
A winning new work of fiction loosely based on events in the life
of anthropologist Margaret Mead. In 1930s Papua New Guinea,
a frustrated British anthropologist meets two colleagues working
in the jungle: Nell, passionate and well respected in the field,
and her mercurial, undisciplined husband, Fen. What unfolds
is at once a steamy love triangle and a nuanced examination of
how scholars study primitive cultures.

Rosemary Mahoney, *Down the Nile: Alone in a Fisherman's Skiff*
The highly entertaining saga of writer and avid oarswoman
Rosemary Mahoney's one-woman trip down the Nile in a
seven-foot rowboat. Hair-raising, humorous, and in the end,
enlightening on the subject of cross-cultural human connections
and friendship, this is travel writing at its best.

Czeslaw Milosz, *New and Collected Poems*
Seven decades of astonishing, transcendent poems from the
Polish poet and winner of the Nobel Prize for Literature. Born in
Lithuania, first published in Poland, driven underground to work
with the Resistance in Paris, Milosz ultimately emigrated to the
United States to teach at Berkeley.

Michael Paterniti, *The Telling Room: A Tale of Love, Betrayal, Revenge, and the World's Greatest Piece of Cheese*

A peripatetic American journalist's ten-year quest to tell the story of Spanish cheese maker Ambrosio Molinos, including the curious saga behind his mystical enterprise in the village of Guzman, Spain.

Audrey Schulman, *Three Weeks in December*

A literary page-turner, interweaving two riveting narratives: a young engineer from Maine who sets off in 1899 to oversee construction of a railroad in East Africa and finds himself the reluctant hunter of two lions preying on his crew's camp; and an American ethnobotanist in Rwanda in 2000, who bonds with a family of endangered gorillas while searching out a rare vine for a lifesaving pharmaceutical. An inspired, seductive read.

Mary Ann Shaffer and Annie Barrows, *The Guernsey Literary and Potato Peel Pie Society*

In 1946 London, writer Juliet Ashton takes up an unlikely correspondence with a man on the isle of Guernsey and is drawn into his eccentric, beguiling, and wonderfully human circle of friends, who pose as a literary society to foil the Germans occupying their island. A real charmer — especially for book clubs!

Janet Wallach, *Desert Queen: The Extraordinary Life of Gertrude Bell: Adventurer, Adviser to Kings, Ally of Lawrence of Arabia*

The story of controversial Victorian aristocrat Gertrude Bell (1868–1926), who explored, mapped, and advised British intelligence on the Arab world during World War I.

on the menu

SOFT FISH TACOS

Conversation is food for the soul.

–Mexican proverb

Growing up in New England in the 1950s and '60s, my exposure to Hispanic cuisine was limited to an exotic side dish called "Spanish rice." As near as I can describe it, it was white rice mixed with some cooked onion, diced red and green peppers, tomato paste, and maybe a few spices. While these ingredients don't sound too bad, or too difficult for you to mix in a skillet, we never made it that way. We bought Spanish rice in a can — inexplicably vacuum-packed, and something like canned tomato-rice soup concentrate, if you upped the rice. Maybe red pepper was too exotic for the local Stop & Shop, or the novelty of America's new love affair with all things precooked, canned, and frozen was too seductive a siren song for most homemakers to resist. All I know is that our Spanish rice required a can opener, and it was usually served with scrambled hamburger meat or stuffed into green-pepper halves and baked to make, well, "stuffed peppers." Seemingly exotic due to being "Spanish," it was a bit of a departure from our meat-and-potatoes diet, and I think I rather liked it.

Moving on. I was introduced to my first taco in the '70s at a friend's apartment in New York City. I was very enthusiastic about all the little bowls of chopped toppings — lettuce, onions, peppers, and tomatoes, plus shredded cheese and salsa. For months afterward, anyone who came to my apartment was served a lavish boxed-taco spread.

Much more recently, my friend, the artist and poet Anita Clearfield, introduced me to fish tacos. Up until then, I'd rather numbly assumed that my old reliable tacos had to have ground beef or maybe shredded chicken as their featured attraction. Not so. Fish tacos are lighter, almost Caribbean, and have been making their way onto casual-restaurant menus everywhere in recent years. Served buffet style, they make a perfect meal for book club nights. The presentation is colorful, the ingredients are healthy, and the results are warming in every sense of the word.

This version of fish tacos features soft tacos and a traditional assortment of vegetable fillings. Californians favor fish tacos made more simply with crisp tortillas, coleslaw, and a kind of chipotle mayonnaise or aioli. They are very good, and if you're pinched for time, try that. But for a group, I like this version with a wider variety of colorful fillings. It makes a fun activity out of your shared meal. However you present them, fish tacos are a perfect light supper for March, when weather is all over the place and food wants to be cheering. Put out red wine sangria and a bowl of corn chips to snack on while you cook the fish, then let everyone make his or her own.

Here's my favorite version of this fun, flexible dish. The preparation looks busy, but it's quite simple; you do the light chopping and prep work ahead of time and place each element in a serving bowl. Just be sure you remember to put all the bowls on the table in the desired state of hot or cold, and no one will grouse. Amounts are approximate — put out as much of each filling as you think your group will consume. You'll need six small to medium (soup-sized) serving bowls and three smaller bowls, plus plenty of serving spoons.

· SOFT FISH TACOS ·

1 large red onion, thinly sliced

1/3 cup good red wine vinegar

Sprinkling of sugar and salt

3 tbsp. olive oil

1/2 tsp. ancho chili powder

1/2 tsp. ground cumin

1 tsp. dried oregano

1 1/2 lbs. filet of flounder, sole, or other flaky white fish

1–2 large avocados, or guacamole*

Sprinkle lime juice

2 medium-sized, firm tomatoes, chopped

2–3 cups combined shredded lettuce and purple cabbage (cabbage shredded very thin)

1 cup canned black beans, rinsed well

1/2 cup salsa

1/2 cup sour cream

10–12 fresh corn tortillas

Lime wedges and sprigs of cilantro, for garnish (optional)
   (Note: some people have a strong aversion to cilantro, so keep it separate.)

*A simple recipe for guacamole is below.

Serves 6

Preparation: Place onions in a small serving bowl. Add red wine vinegar and sprinkling of sugar and salt, and set on the table for 60 minutes (or more) to marinate. (This can also be made a day ahead and covered tightly in the fridge.)

Whisk the olive oil with chili powder, cumin, and oregano, and pour it over the fish in a nonreactive dish. Set to marinate at least 30 minutes in the refrigerator before cooking.

If using guacamole, prepare it ahead of time from the recipe below and refrigerate in a small serving bowl to set out just before serving. Otherwise, pare and chop a large avocado or two, sprinkle with lime juice, and wrap to prevent browning.

Place chopped tomatoes, lettuce/cabbage mixture, rinsed beans, salsa, and sour cream in separate bowls and set out on the table. Stack serving plates buffet style.

10 minutes before serving: Place tortillas directly on rack in a warm (300°F, or 150°C) oven.

Heat a nonstick frying pan over medium-high heat. Remove fish from marinade and place in pan; cook approximately 3 minutes a side. Remove fish onto a small platter and flake the fish with its pan juices for serving. Garnish with lime wedges and cilantro sprigs, if desired.

Homemade guacamole: Wash and remove the stem navel from 2 avocados. Run a sharp knife around the fruit's circumference lengthwise, pressing the blade against the pit. Twist and pull to separate in half. Set the halves on a cutting board and slice each again lengthwise into quarters. Carefully pull the quarter sections away from the half with the pit.

With the avocado cut in quarters, peel back the skin. If the avocados are overripe, you may need to scoop flesh out with a spoon. (Note: a few brown streaks in a ripe avocado are just a sign of bruising, and the flesh is still fine to eat. However, if the avocado is badly discolored, it will be bitter. If you see any signs of mold, or if the flesh is stringy, don't try to use it.) Put the clear flesh of the avocado into a small, deep bowl. With a hand chopper, chop and mash the avocados until only small chunks are visible. Add the juice of 1 lemon, $\frac{1}{2}$ teaspoon sea salt, 3 tablespoons salsa, and 2 tablespoons sour cream. Continue to blend, and check for seasoning. Refrigerate until ready to serve.

APRIL/FUNNY PAGES

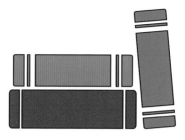

The good ended happily, and the bad unhappily.
That is what Fiction means.

–Oscar Wilde, *The Importance of Being Earnest*

DO YOU REMEMBER the first book that made you laugh out loud? I don't mean joke books or comic strips (which, come to think of it, are never really funny at any age), but real human, situational, and contextual humor. For me, it was *The Catcher in the Rye*. I was 14 and reading it, nonstop, late into the night by flashlight under the covers in the bedroom I shared with my sister. Holden Caulfield made me laugh. He was jaded and irreverent, and cursed like a sailor — and I adored him. I was bereft when I finished the book. Of course, I didn't know then that the book was a literary tour de force, destined to become an American classic — it just struck me as funny. I've read it many times over since then, and it still makes me laugh. And now, maybe cry a little too. It also showed me at a young age that brilliant literature can be humorous. Mark Twain helped me there. And later, under the tutelage of a good English teacher, even Shakespeare.

As young people living in New York City in the '70s and '80s, my friends and I embraced the debut of John Irving's comic novels, starting with *The World According to Garp*. Irving gave us a kind of lovely escapism to crazy families joyfully scrapped together from pieces of broken-and-mended-back-together people. The books had human mascots and pet bears. The plots meandered irrationally, punctuated by big, laugh-out-loud scenes. When Irving sets up a scene, like the one in *The Hotel New Hampshire* with the grandfather, barbells, and dog on rollers (I'll say no more, so no spoiler alert needed — if you've read it, you know what I mean), it is every bit as satisfying as any meticulously timed and choreographed comedy scene on film or TV — better, really.

Later I discovered the unhinged hilarity of Carl Hiaasen's novels, and, with my first *New Yorker* subscription, David Sedaris's pitch-perfect, self-deprecating wit. Both are the kind of writers whose early work was so good, I didn't think they could keep it up. But I was wrong. Sedaris, who first captured our hearts with his essay "SantaLand Diaries," chronicling the madness of a job stint as a Macy's Christmas elf, just kept getting better. And as I write, my husband is reading Carl Hiaasen's brand-new 12th novel, *Bad Monkey*, some 20-plus years after he read the first one. I can hear him downstairs chuckling his way through it. These literary funnymen have legs.

To read a book requires us to participate. Once set down on paper, the words of a story are always the same. It is we, as readers, who breathe life, vitality, and human emotion — love, anger, sorrow, or delight — into those words. Most avid readers are happy to imagine the voices of their favorite characters without actually hearing them speak. So much so that sometimes seeing a movie version can be totally disconcerting. I experienced that disconnect when I saw the film *Simon Birch*, based loosely on Irving's *A Prayer for Owen Meany*. I adored that book and heard Owen's high-pitched CAPITAL LETTER speech so clearly in my head, there was no way the physical actor on screen could embody the role.

If performance comedy is all about timing, then great comic writing has to be, at least in part, about phrasing and word choice. Some words are funny: *Chicken* is funny. *Hen* is not. *Underwear* is funny, underpants not. *Noodle* yes, *pasta* no. How you roll out your punch line has to be perfect. Veteran comedians cite the infallibility of one classic joke: *When I die, I want to go peacefully like my grandfather did — in his sleep. Not yelling and screaming like the passengers in his backseat.* And that's a joke about a car accident.

In the best comic novels and nonfiction works, humor arises from context and character. Their authors have a very specialized toolbox: understatement (meiosis), overstatement (hyperbole), satire, and sarcasm can all bring to the task. When the writing is good, these devices are invisible. Writers give their characters dialects, idiosyncratic diction, and all manner of quirks to make us chuckle. They are put in situations they have no idea how to handle. We watch them use their wits — or lack of — to come out the other side. Part of us can identify with the hapless character, or with those who have to deal with him — it's life with all its banana peels, and we relate to it. There is an old adage that writing comedy is far more difficult than writing drama. If you've ever been assigned to pen the class skit or a witty toast, you know how painfully true that is.

april reads

It's my personal opinion that there are not enough comic novels published anymore. There are a lot of humorous memoirs and essays, but, at the risk of sounding like the late Andy Rooney, I sometimes think we could use more wit and less angst in American literature. Americans are funny. American life is funny. Yet we often take ourselves very seriously in the supposedly elevated world of arts and letters. That said, there are many, many wonderful laugh-out-loud books to be read — the best will also make you tear up a bit too. They say real belly laughter is good for your health. Here are a few of my favorite health tips.

Alan Bennett, *The Uncommon Reader*
British playwright Alan Bennett's charming and irreverent tribute to books and the joys of reading. A fictional Queen Elizabeth II wanders into a mobile library van in search of her runaway corgis, where, enamored with the freedoms of unfettered reading choices, she becomes an avid reader — to the dismay of her ministers and at the expense of her royal duties. A small charmer laced with light political and literary satire.

Bill Bryson, *The Life and Times of the Thunderbolt Kid*
Bryson's joyously unfettered memoir of growing up in the American Midwest in the 1950s, complete with hijinks at county fairs, church suppers, and baseball games, and in the family living room.

Helen Fielding, *Bridget Jones's Diary*
Initially a hugely popular newspaper column in London's *The Independent*, this is the full one-year diary of 30-something Bridget Jones that became a Hollywood vehicle for Renée Zellweger. As she obsesses over her weight, love life, meddling mother, and food, drink, and cigarette intake (and makes constant resolutions for self-improvement), Bridget is the lovable screwup everyone can relate to.

Carl Hiaasen, *Tourist Season*

The veteran Miami columnist's first novel and one of his best. Through rogue reporter Skip Wiley, Hiaasen takes bold aim at land developers, politics, corruption, and ecological destruction, which will become the signature themes of his many darkly humorous and antic best-sellers set in the Florida Panhandle.

David Sedaris, *Me Talk Pretty One Day*

A collection of 27 humorous essays by the masterful satirist and observer of human foibles — mostly his own. Many of these stories chronicle Sedaris's ragged attempts to speak fluent French as a recent transplant to Paris, but they also range widely from his quirky childhood family to the confounding task of navigating daily adult life. Not surprisingly, Sedaris claims over seven million books in print, in dozens of languages.

Maria Semple, *Where'd You Go, Bernadette*

A hilarious and heartwarming romp starring Bernadette, an architect, wife, and private school mom in trendy Seattle, who is so fed up with helicopter parents, her exhaustingly eco-conscious neighbors, and TED talks, that she disappears. In a nontraditional narrative of e-mails, correspondence, and even FBI documents, her inventive daughter, Bee, tries to find her mother. A tour de force of modern satire from the accomplished television writer.

Kevin Wilson, *The Family Fang*

A brilliant, ambitious, and laugh-out-loud novel of art, artists, and family life. The Fang parents are out-there performance artists. Their children (known as Child A and Child B) are unwilling players in their parents' chaotic world of freewheeling artistic expression. With this razor-sharp comic novel, the Fang family takes its place alongside those *Tenenbaums* and other paragons of zany family dysfunction.

on the menu

SPRING GREENS

Animals that sleep in the winter emerge with
most of their fat gone, and then refresh themselves with
tonic weeds and berries before the strenuous mating season.
Men are less obvious than this, but still feel an atavistic
hunger for green leaves in the spring.

–M. F. K. Fisher, *A Cordiall Water*

Not everyone has access to wild asparagus, and most people I
grew up with considered dandelion greens a front-lawn menace to
be confronted with an arsenal of pesticides. Still, we are learning,
and more and more of us are trying to teach our bodies to follow
the rhythm of the seasons in choosing what we eat. Folk medicine
has always held that humans need to purge their sluggish winter
systems in spring with thin broths, acidic waters, and bitter greens.
And at least for a short duration, such a regimen would likely
benefit most of us.

In recent years, we have elected to support several neighborhood
CSAs (community supported agriculture cooperatives). Not only
does our early buy-in support these hardworking local farmers,
but it also gives us a sense of being vested in their enterprise. We
become loyal customers when the farm stand is full, and in this way
have made the acquaintance of many new and delicious greens
and vegetables over the years — not to mention some like-minded
neighbors. Growing up in mill-town Massachusetts, iceberg lettuce
and Birds Eye frozen vegetables were the closest we came to leafy

greens for most of the calendar year. I could never have imagined I would someday be dining blissfully on the likes of tatsoi, kohlrabi, pea shoots, black kale, pale green towers of romanesco, tomatillos, gorgeous fuchsia watermelon radishes, ten kinds of baby salad greens, and edible flowers. We all know that most small children need to be coaxed into an amiable relationship with green vegetables. But I know any number of baby boomers who seem permanently conditioned by their greens-free childhoods and still eye with dread a plate of steamed kale or chard. When I know I will be cooking for them, I become furtive. I've tried chopping my greens fine and folding them into cheese, cream, and herbs for a delectable baked gratin, or hiding them in pasta stirred with plenty of bacon or sausage. But my ruse is invariably outed. The scars from frozen succotash and gray-green canned peas can apparently be deep and lasting. I keep trying, though. Do not come to my house for lunch or dinner and expect to be spared my missionary zeal to bring what my husband calls "scratchy greens" abundantly into your life.

A few summers ago, I invited an old college friend and her 20-something-year-old daughter to lunch. It was a lovely day, and I set our table outside in the yard. My friend had been an admirable activist in numerous liberal grassroots causes in her day, and now works as an artist. I hadn't seen her in many years and had never met her daughter. It seemed logical to surmise that one or both might be vegetarian, and I'd better play it safe with the lunch menu. I made a pretty caprese salad of ripe garden tomatoes, basil, and fresh mozzarella drizzled with olive oil. I laid out smoked trout with lemon slices on a big platter lined with arugula, fresh dill, and thin-sliced cucumbers with a little dish of tangy mayonnaise dressing. And I warmed up crusty olive bread rolls for the four of us. We sat down to our lunch with a cold bottle of wine and some iced tea. I noticed the daughter eyeing the platters nervously as she patted, but did not eat, the bread on her plate. I encouraged her to help herself to the salad and trout. "Oh, I don't eat vegetables," she said, "only meat." I was unprepared for this. A Paleo ahead of her time? The daughter finally ate a slice or two of mozzarella, and I scared up some hard salami from the fridge for her. Someone didn't like olives. The iced tea was popular. I drank the wine.

How people live — never mind eat — without a nod to the bounty of gardens is an anathema to me. I could not function without regular rations of spinach or chard or broccoli rabe. I do not want to envision a world without arugula or basil. But after a winter of even the best root vegetables, kales, and cabbages, those first greens of the spring season are curative. One way to serve up these welcome but sometimes slightly bitter spring greens is to cook them with eggs. Folded into an omelet or strata, dark greens make a deliciously complex match for the rich, creamy eggs. The strata preparation I will give you here is a stable, make-ahead version of an omelet with spring greens and is perfect for a light evening meal. It is also perfect for a weekend brunch and is fail-safe, so you can focus your energies on the more crucial task of making Bloody Marys. The strata is meant to be assembled the night before, so the bread soaks up the custard mixture overnight. Or, if you make it the day of your gathering, be sure to give it at least four hours in the fridge before cooking. With plenty of cheese to keep it moist, leftovers (if you have any) can be reheated briefly in a 350°F (175°C) oven for a quick lunch or pickup supper.

• STRATA WITH ASPARAGUS AND SPRING GREENS •

2 tbsp. butter, plus more for greasing pan

8–10 slices of good bread, cut about 1/2" thick (You can use sourdough, whole wheat, English muffin bread, or any other tasty bread — and day old is even better than fresh.)

6 eggs

3 cups milk

Dash nutmeg

1/2 tsp. salt

White pepper, to taste

1/2 cup chopped green onions

2 cups baby spinach

1 cup arugula or sorrel

1/4 cup chopped fresh chives

1 1/2 cups shredded Gruyère or cheddar cheese

1 lb. small asparagus spears, blanched and cut into 2" lengths (about 2–3 cups)

Serves 6

Preparation: Butter a 9"x12" baking dish and line with half the bread slices, cutting slices as needed to fit the pan, and set aside.

Beat eggs and milk well, add nutmeg, salt, and pepper, and set aside. Melt 2 tablespoons butter in a large frying pan and add green onions. Cook over medium-high heat until soft but not brown. Add spinach, arugula and chives. Fold to mix with onions and wilt slightly. Remove immediately from heat.

To assemble: Spread the sautéed greens and half the cheese over the bread in the baking dish. Add the second layer of bread slices to cover, cutting to fit pan as needed. Arrange the blanched asparagus pieces over this layer. Pour the egg mixture over the top and sprinkle with remaining cheese. Press down on the top to make sure all the bread gets soaked with the egg mixture.

Cover and refrigerate overnight, or at least 4 hours. Bake at 350°F (175°C) for about 45 minutes, or until golden and puffy. Let stand 10 minutes before serving. The beauty of strata is that it can be made the day before and will cook up perfectly up to 24 hours later. Any mix of vegetables (such as mushrooms, red pepper, and broccoli) or meats, if desired (bacon, sausage, etc.), and other types of cheese can also be used in this dish. Just be sure to have at least 3 cups filling and 1½ cups cheese.

If you want an accompaniment, you might serve this strata with a simple plate of early tomatoes — mix red vine, plum, yellow, cherry, and whatever your greengrocer has available. A drizzle of olive oil and a few grinds of fresh pepper are all they need.

MAY/ESSAYS AND MEMOIR

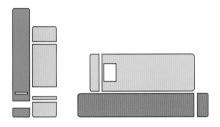

You must know that there is nothing higher, stronger,
more wholesome, and more useful for one's future life
than some good memory, especially one carried
from childhood, from one's family home.

—Fyodor Dostoevsky, *The Brothers Karamazov*

MOST OF US succumb to that kind of blissful daffiness we call
"spring fever" when the air at last begins to soften and trees finally
burst into pink and white blossoms. There is probably a medical or
neurological explanation for it, having to do with olfactory pleasure
centers or the brain's response to heat and light after months
of near hibernation, but we really don't need one. Just about
everyone can remember clock watching in a classroom, staring out
windows filled with newly bright afternoon sun. College students
and young lovers moon around on sidewalks or sprawl on the
greening lawns. Everyone seems to have a recital, prom, or picnic
in the offing. Brides plan weddings. The countdown to summer
vacation days begins.

And so, how curious but also true it is that when the days become warm and full of promise, we contrarian humans can't resist looking back. The past floods in on the first scent of new-cut grass or a gardenia wrist corsage, or the sight of a watery rainbow in a bell of garden-hose spray. I can smell — yes, it had a scent — the crepe paper we used for making May baskets (if you don't know what a May basket is, don't worry — you're in the overwhelming majority) or wrapping it around bicycle handlebars for the school parade. Someone would weave a deck of cards into the wheel spokes, so that they made a crazy fluttering sound as you rode. It can be maddening, this realization that up to the age of about ten or 12, we are all sponges. Nothing is too minute to deposit in the memory bank. And there it stays, indelible and reverberating for decades. After that . . . well, it can get a bit murky.

It's good to know we have company. The art of the memoir or personal essay, for better or worse, has never been more popular or more generously published. While autobiography is generally considered to be the true story of a life, memoir encompasses all manner of recollected stories from a life. MFA programs across the country now teach the skillful exposition of personal memories and narratives, and every celebrity with 15 or 20 minutes of fame to claim has written (or delivered an "as told to" version of) at least some meaty nuggets from his or her saga. The majority of these efforts have limited audiences, to say the least. But the best are richly rewarding literary achievements. There is no substitute for the immediacy and candor of an engaging first-person narrative in the hands of a skilled writer. Whether their authors have served as prime ministers or chambermaids, first-person accounts that are well told invariably find an audience. These memoirs are the vessels in which our histories are carried forward in time, survive us, and enable us to share our hard-won human experience with those who come after us. The practice of documenting life stories is as ancient as civilization itself. Julius Caesar set down his *Commentaries* on the Gallic Wars in 49 BC. The artist Benvenuto Cellini wrote his famous vita in the 1550s, and Ben Franklin's unfinished memoir was published in 1790. In modern times, the autobiographical urge is programmed into us at an early age. Schoolchildren are assigned to write down "what I did on my summer vacation" and share it with the class. For some, this is little more than an open invitation to lie blatantly about wondrous exploits that never occurred (thus novelists are born). Others actually tell the truth about swimming in the pond (twice), walking the neighbor's dog for cash, or sitting around eating Popsicles and watching TV with equally idle friends. Before long, some language arts teacher wants you to write about your life — all 12 years of it — and illustrate it with scrapbook photos. Voila: you've written a personal essay. And this is all before the college application wants you to write about your most transformative human experience.

Short nonfiction that is not strictly journalism, reportage, or research is sometimes referred to as "creative nonfiction." Within the genre can be found additional subcategories, such as autobiographical, personal, or lyric essay; humorous essay; segmented essay; review, critique, op-ed, or social commentary; epistolary essay; travelogue and food writing; and dozens of other variants on the genre. I recently heard the term "fictional essay" — presumably one where the bones of the story are factual, but the author has added invented context, dialogue, and behaviors. There are shadings within these classifications, and sometimes (e.g., *A Million Little Pieces*) a major literary kerfuffle arises over what is fact and what is fiction.

may reads

The New Yorker's "The Talk of the Town" immortalized a generation of writers who mastered the short essay in all its richness during the golden age of Lillian Ross's editorship. It gave us Thurber, White, Trillin, Angell, and Updike. More recently, we are dazzled by the perspicacious talents of essayists such as Adam Gopnik and Patricia Marx. Traditionally, newspapers, periodicals, and literary journals provided the primary forums for the American essay and served as springboards to launch the careers of talented writers. With the growth of the Internet, the short essay in all its variety has flourished. Online journals, e-zines, interactive Web sites, blogs, and myriad electronic forums are ever ravenous for content. That does not mean all of it is good — quite the contrary. Still, there are wonderful works out there, and reconnecting with personal narratives by first-rate writers is a balm to the disaffected. In its simplest form, it is the *art of telling our stories*. At its most essential and human level, that art will never grow stale. Here are some winning memoirs and essay collections that will not disappoint.

Russell Baker, *Growing Up*
> The Pulitzer Prize–winning humorist and master wordsmith's beguiling account of growing up in the '30s and '40s in rural Virginia. Baker, who lost his father when he was five years old, pays literary tribute to his mother and her unflagging faith in her young son's writing talent in this memorable coming-of-age story.

Roz Chast, *Can't We Talk About Something More Pleasant?*
> New Yorker cartoonist Roz Chast's remarkable graphic memoir of coping with the decline of her aged parents. With characteristic wit and insight, Chast chronicles the surreal transition from only child to parenting her parents. Chast's handwritten text and

signature artwork cover leaving the family home crammed with memorabilia, moving her parents in their 90s into institutional care, dealing with caregivers, and finally, the life-altering loss of parents. Comic and heartbreaking, this unique book is a must-read for anyone coping with the care of elderly parents.

Jill Ker Conway, *The Road from Coorain*
From a harsh life on the family sheep farm in the Australian outback, to attending school in wartime Sydney, to becoming president of Smith College and an esteemed national leader in U.S. academic circles, this is Conway's inspiring story of tenacity and personal determination.

Joan Didion, *The White Album*
Literary journalist Joan Didion's 1979 montage of American social change fomenting in the late '60s and early '70s. With arresting detail and precision, Didion digs beneath the surface of the women's movement, the Manson Family murders, the Black Panther Party, and student agitation on California college campuses, among other mass-culture upheavals of the time.

M. F. K. Fisher, *As They Were*
A superb collection of essays by the brilliant epicure, world traveler, and writer extraordinaire, tracking her travels from her hometown of Whittier, California, to time spent in her beloved France and the Provence regions.

Mary Karr, *The Liars' Club*
Poet Mary Karr's groundbreaking 1995 memoir of growing up in a hardscrabble Texas oil town. Funny, raw, and deeply affecting, Karr's book — the first in her autobiographical series — is credited with inspiring a resurgence in the personal memoir.

Maxine Kumin, *Women, Animals, and Vegetables*
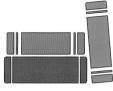
Earthy and informed essays on just these topics,
by the late Pulitzer Prize–winning poet. From her
farm in New Hampshire, Kumin reflects on her
life as an accomplished horsewoman, farmer, and naturalist —
a life lived, she claims, as an antidote to the heady business of
poetry.

Kim Dana Kupperman, *I Just Lately Started Buying Wings*
The title essay will charm you. The others will astonish you with
their literary and emotional rigor. Kupperman is a fearless explorer
of damaged and broken lives that still cannot resist seeking
redemption. Discerning readers will want to meet this brilliant new
voice in American letters.

Anna Quindlen, *Thinking Out Loud*
The best of the *New York Times* opinion columnist Anna
Quindlen's smart, passionate writings on everything from the
Anita Hill congressional hearings to gays in the military and the
trials of raising children in the modern age. A breath of fresh
air for women and men everywhere, especially on those days
American life seems to have run amok.

Penelope Schwartz Robinson, *Slippery Men*
Winner of the Stonecoast Book Prize. Judge Katha Pollitt writes
of this superb essay collection and its author: "Both women
and men will smile at themselves in the mirror she holds up to
contemporary life."

Dustin Beall Smith, *Key Grip: A Memoir of Endless Consequences*
Winner of the 2007 Bakeless Prize for nonfiction from the
Breadloaf Writers' Conference at Middlebury College. Smith's
work is lauded by Robert Atwan, series editor of Best American
Essays, as "one of the best memoirs I've read in years." Author
Susan Isaacs writes: "*Key Grip* is nonstop pleasure."

Monica Wood, *When We Were the Kennedys*

Maine author Monica Wood's wry and affecting memoir of her family of four girls growing up in the mill town of Mexico, Maine. When their father unexpectedly dies in 1963, the family finds its own loss mirroring that of the nation's first family in the wake of the Kennedy assassination. A pitch-perfect memoir of one family and one nation's passage through loss and recovery in a turbulent era of American life.

Baron Wormser, *The Road Washes Out in Spring*

Poet Baron Wormser's keen observations and eloquent account of living "off the grid" with his young family in rural Maine, with no electricity or running water for 25 years. These essays comprise a profound contemplation on the nature of isolation and community, self-sufficiency, contentment, poetry, and the ways in which we expend our energies in a modern world.

on the menu

SALAD NIÇOISE

Of all main-course salads, the niçoise is my all-time
favorite, with its fresh butter-lettuce foundation;
its carefully cooked, beautifully green green beans;
its colorful contrast of halved hard-boiled eggs,
ripe red tomatoes, and black olives; all fortified
by chunks of tuna fish and freshly opened anchovies . . .
— an inspired combination that pleases everyone.

–Julia Child, *Julia's Kitchen Wisdom*

When my mother was growing up in a small Maine city on the
Kennebec River, she never ate a salad. Or rather, I should say,
never ate a green salad of lettuces or raw vegetables. She was
not deprived; were she here, she would have me hasten to assure
you that her mother was an excellent home cook for the day. This
meant well-done meats, potatoes, cream sauces, stuffings galore,
cooked vegetables that had long ago given up their chlorophyll, and
lots and lots of sugar: cookies of every description, elaborate cakes
and pies, puddings, and that lethal concoction known as "fudge."

My father's family members, on the other hand, were horse
and farm people. They grew vegetables in their own garden and
consumed them in quantity. On one of her first visits to the Browns'
Massachusetts home sometime in the 1940s, my mother observed
her future in-laws setting out a large bowl of torn-up lettuce. It
might as well have been the backyard — she had no idea what
to do with it. And she was not alone. Such was the state of the

American palate for much of the middle class before giant supermarkets, Julia, organic farmers, Whole Foods, CSAs, and local food sourcing. It was also before the advent of the more troubling trends of agribusiness, GMOs, and — as we all began to travel the world by air, sampling and then demanding exotic foreign fare — the impacts of globalization and long-haul food importation.

Thanks to my father's early influence, and because our culinary times have so dramatically evolved, I adore salads. I love them cold and vinegary on a hot day, or savory with warm vegetables and goat cheese in the fall. I love cabbages and root vegetables, shredded into slaws tossed with sweet-sour dressings. I can even be talked into some salads with strawberries or peaches, though I admit to suffering flashbacks to those cling peach and canned pear arrangements, and I approach fruit additions to salads warily. Except blood oranges and dried cranberries or pomegranate seeds in a salad of dark greens at Christmas, which is one of my favorite things to serve. Throw in a few toasted pecans, and you have a healthful red-and-green creation to lighten your holiday meals.

I probably ordered my first chef's salad at some restaurant on Massachusetts's North Shore — maybe in one of the old summer hotels where we sometimes went for a special lunch on my birthday. I know I was intrigued by its "arranged-ness": the uniformly thin-sliced julienne of ham, turkey, and Swiss cheese. I ate my first Cobb salad at an expensive, old-world restaurant on Newbury Street in Boston, where a teenage friend and I had gone for a special day of shopping, after dashing inside for cover from a sudden rainstorm at lunchtime. Once through the heavy oaken door, it was unavoidable that we enter the hushed dining room. By the spotless white linens and sparkling silver, we immediately knew we were in over our financial heads. Neither of our menus had prices on it since we were both given "ladies' menus," so we had to ask our waiter — who was very discreet and, I suspect, more than a little amused — what the food cost. We searched for the cheapest dish we could find and sipped our water. We ordered just one Cobb salad to share between us and barely had enough money to pay our check. But I remembered well the wonderful mélange of chicken, avocado, bacon, and chopped egg brought to our table by our solicitous waiter. It was delicious, and we felt very adult in our fine restaurant eating Cobb salad. Impoverished, but adult. I expect our waiter did not receive much in the way of a tip for all his kind attentions to us. Someone later told me the mnemonic EAT COBB to remember the ingredients: egg, avocado, tomato, chicken, onion, bacon, blue cheese.

I do not remember when I was first introduced to salad niçoise. It might have been during college at a tavern in town, or even in Europe on my junior year abroad program. I do know that it was instantly my favorite salad, and I ordered it everywhere I went for years. I loved its vibrant colors and the odd combination of small, cold potatoes, tomatoes, crisp string beans, chunk tuna, and salty little olives splashed with lemon and olive oil. Before it is disturbed, it is beautiful to look at, and it tastes every bit as good as it looks.

Here is a salad niçoise for a warm May evening. This is, more or less, Julia Child's preparation for a basic niçoise. After all, who better than The French Chef to take the lead in defining this classic French salad, reputedly originating in Nice and so named for the small, black olives that are one of its critical ingredients? She does something with shallots that I don't bother with, and I have always loved to add chickpeas to this hearty, complex salad, though they are not required in the classic version. I also use a good base of chopped

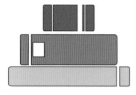

romaine when serving for a group, as that lovely, soft butter lettuce she espouses fairly disappears after the dressing hits it. This is definitely a warm-weather menu, though some restaurants serve this salad with chunks of fresh, grilled tuna steak year-round. If you were to offer up your niçoise on a chilly night, I would recommend comforting your guests with a piping hot soup as well. Something light, like a clear-broth mushroom soup or even consommé with lemon would do. Heat the bread (and your dining room) and hope for the best. Salad niçoise and most salads *composée* are best suited to warm-weather dining.

The secret to preparing this salad efficiently for a midday or evening meal is to cook and chill the eggs, green beans, and potatoes in the morning, and to make the dressing ahead. I even chop the parsley in advance, so the dinner salad assembly is relatively simple. However you approach it, arrange the ingredients on top of the greens like a pie chart, so your guests can see and select the elements they favor. This way, there is no need to isolate the anchovies for those tender palates with an aversion — poor souls — and the salad will also be beautiful to behold. Or, if you have especially squeamish guests, by all means, serve the little salty fish on a separate plate or leave them out altogether. A little license is a good thing to take.

Julia dresses certain elements ahead, but I prefer my salad undressed until the very last minute — just put out a good mustardy vinaigrette on the side, and let everyone dress his or her own.

· SALAD NIÇOISE ·

1 large head Boston lettuce, washed and dried
1 large head romaine lettuce, washed and dried
½ lb. green beans, ends snipped, blanched, and chilled
2–4 firm tomatoes, cut in wedges, or 12 large cherry tomatoes, halved
6–8 small new potatoes, boiled in skin and chilled
1 cup canned chickpeas, rinsed well in cold water and well drained
6 hard-boiled eggs, peeled and cut in half
1 can anchovy fillets
½ cup small, black niçoise-type olives
6 oz. canned Italian tuna, packed in olive oil
Fresh ground pepper
2–3 tbsp. capers
Finely chopped leaf parsley, to garnish

Serves 6

Dressing *(Make ahead)***:** Whisk juice of 1 large lemon (about ¼ cup) with 1 teaspoon salt until foamy. Whisk in 1 tablespoon Dijon mustard. Slowly whisk in ¾ cup extra-virgin olive oil until emulsified. Add a few grinds fresh black pepper, and blend well. Serve at room temperature.

Preparation: Tear Boston lettuce and coarsely chop romaine. Heap into a large salad bowl and mix. In pie-shaped wedges, arrange green beans, tomatoes, potatoes, chickpeas, eggs, anchovies, and olives on top of greens, arranging colors to make an attractive presentation. Flake tuna in a pile in the center. Grind fresh pepper over salad and sprinkle with capers and chopped parsley. Serve with slices of fresh, warmed baguette and dressing on the side.

JUNE / LITERARY FICTION

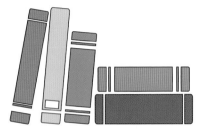

Summer afternoon – summer afternoon;
to me those have always been the two most
beautiful words in the English language.

–Henry James

IF YOU ARE very lucky, you grew up with plenty of storybooks and caring family and friends who read them aloud to you. It used to be that town librarians were sent around like traveling performers to sit in front of classrooms, awkwardly holding picture books open while peering around the cover to read the story aloud. I met Mike Mulligan and his wonderful steam shovel in this manner, and the villagers who made stone soup from a rock and a turnip. Our visiting librarian, who looked like Maria Von Trapp's mother, with her dirndl skirt and a long, gray braid wrapped and pinned around her head, read in a kind of trilling, overly enthusiastic voice that made us all a little nervous. But for the many children in our melting-pot town whose weary parents rarely or never had time for reading aloud, I think our elderly shepherdess of a librarian was heaven-sent.

As we become readers, we are also learning to form written words. For some of us, it is irresistible not to imitate those who make the magic of storybooks. A writer friend told me that when he was young, his mother worked in a coffee shop. The first story he ever wrote involved a unicorn who went to work at a very similar establishment, but didn't fit in, not being able to pour coffee or clear dishes. But one day (there is always "one day" in our early narratives), the unicorn found his niche serving doughnuts onto customers' plates via his singular horn. It was called "The Unicorn in the Coffee Shop." And somewhere, folded away in a scrapbook, I have a story I wrote around the time I was in first grade, called "The Littlest Child at the Party." Being short of stature myself at age six (and ever after), I penned this righteous fable where all the children at a party are exhorted to play pin the tail on the donkey. The littlest girl cannot reach the donkey, but later on (there is always "later on") they play some game involving crawling under things, where our diminutive narrator excels.

For those who go on writing, who study and work to hone their craft, there is sometimes a moment — a kind of clicking into place — when they *think* they *might* want to become a writer. My first poetry writing class was held in the dank front parlor of a charmless student hotel in southwest London. I was 19 and on a junior year abroad program. I consigned my long winter afternoons to a cadaverous and excitingly named Scottish poet instructor, George MacBeth, and prepared to be mortally humiliated. Four months later, I thought I had found my life's calling. In his hypnotic brogue, George read us the modern poets: Yeats, Auden, Larkin, Thomas, and Eliot. He gave us writing prompts and dared us to hear our own mermaids singing. I wrote parodies of famous works. I wrote poems of my youth as if it were over. I wrote poems of unrequited love for anyone I met. And for a whole month, I wrote interminable epics and ballads. George assigned me haiku as therapy.

Reading those poets for the first time, and taking my initial tentative steps as a fledgling writer of poems, I was uncharacteristically studious that winter. I'd been a respectable but never passionate student, so no one was more surprised than I to find myself in the throes of a new fascination with language and what I could do with it. To this day, I can place myself in that shabby little hotel lounge, sprawled on the garish carpet with my classmates, listening to George MacBeth, perched like a gangly scarecrow, pipe-cleaner legs wound around the spools of his chair, waving a bony hand in the air for emphasis as he intoned magnificent poems to us.

As with those poems, there are books that linger on in the place where they were first read — the summer camp where you spent every rest hour devouring *Gone with the Wind*. The week at the beach house recovering from a tonsillectomy, then reading *The Lord of the Rings* till three in the morning. Every year that we are able to take a winter vacation in the tropics, I devour two or three or four books on the plane and the beach. They are as much a part of the vacation as where we stay or what we see or where we dine. The books themselves become woven into the fabric of our holiday.

june reads

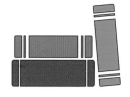

I know where I was when I read every one of the
following books. They possessed me for days. I walked
to the store or climbed the stairs as if I were their protagonists — I observed
myself and my actions in the narrative voices of the novels. I entered these
novels and lived in their worlds till the final page and beyond. Some are
critically acclaimed and honored. Some are quietly accomplished. The
publishing industry, the *académie*, and booksellers like to make distinctions
between "literary" fiction and "popular" (or "pop") fiction, though the lines
can be more than a little blurred. Some great literature becomes hugely
popular. Some genre fiction rises to the level of great literature. I don't
put too much stock in the categories, but the books listed here are likely
to be found on the "Fiction" shelves of your bookstore, or possibly some
adjacent shelving that, for reasons not exactly clear to anyone, will be tagged
"Literature." In any case, all are engaging stories by masterful storytellers that
will take you to new places and bring some fine literary company to be your
summer house guests. Brilliant, tragic, courageous, or simply human, these
characters are easy keepers. Like Marianne Moore's "superior people" from
her poem "Silence," they are self-reliant visitors who never "have to be shown
Longfellow's grave/or the glass flowers at Harvard." And best of all, after they
leave you have your book club — you can talk about them.

James Agee, *A Death in the Family*
    Opening with Agee's achingly beautiful prologue "Knoxville:
    Summer of 1915," a powerful, autobiographical novel of familial
    loss and survival. An American masterpiece of lyric narrative.

Margaret Atwood, *The Handmaid's Tale*
    One of Canadian author Margaret Atwood's most popular and
    chilling works of speculative fiction. In a dystopian future, women

are robbed of all power and dignity, serving only as reproductive "handmaids" for a government of theocratic dictators. A provocative tour de force.

Tracy Chevalier, *Girl with a Pearl Earring*
The vividly imagined backstory of Dutch master Johannes Vermeer's mysterious portrait of a turbaned young woman wearing a pearl earring. Rich in period texture and domestic details of the artist's likely life in 1660s Delft, the book was adapted for a Hollywood film.

Andre Dubus III, *House of Sand and Fog*
A former commander under the deposed Iranian Shah defects to the United States, where he struggles to make a new life. While secretly consigned to menial labor, he must maintain an illusion of success and prosperity for his wife and marriageable daughter, with tragic consequences. A haunting and insightful novel of hubris and the human quest for dignity.

Louise Erdrich, *The Round House*
From the celebrated chronicler of Native American life, Erdrich's exquisitely written, suspenseful page-turner of an Ojibwe boy's coming of age on a reservation in the wake of a racist attack on his mother. Winner of the 2012 National Book Award, the novel has often been described as the Native American *To Kill a Mockingbird*.

Jeffrey Eugenides, *Middlesex*
One of the first major novels to explore the emotional mysteries of gender identity, *Middlesex* is an expansive narrative, as it traces 80 years in the life of a Greek American family, as narrated by his endearing protagonist, Cal (née Calliope) Stephanides. Tracking medical, psychological, and social history in the latter half of 20th-century America, this is a prescient and deeply compassionate literary triumph.

Sue Monk Kidd, *The Secret Life of Bees*

A tenderhearted coming-of-age story in which 14-year-old Lily, dislocated by a murky family history, lands in the gentle world of a beekeeping family of sisters in 1960s South Carolina and is set to work making "Black Madonna" honey. Lily and a parade of memorable female characters arrive at a place of spiritual awakening and reckoning in this beloved novel of magical realism, rooted in the Southern gothic tradition.

Jhumpa Lahiri, *The Namesake*

Afflicted with the awkward name of a Russian writer, second-generation immigrant Gogol Ganguli struggles to find his place in the world. Belonging to neither the tradition-bound birth culture of his parents in Calcutta, nor the family's conflicted experience assimilating into modern American life in Cambridge, Massachusetts, Gogol stumbles through a clash of cultures, generational expectations, comic detours, and misbegotten love affairs, to discover his own unique identity.

Toni Morrison, *Beloved*

Morrison's masterful tale of slavery, secrets, and spirits who return to bear witness. Set in antebellum Ohio, the book is heralded as her personal masterpiece. Morrison's steady, lyrical prose peels back layers of grief and silent histories, leading to the novel's explosive and inevitable finale.

Ann Patchett, *Bel Canto*

Politics, peril, friendships, and passions intertwine when a group of guests — including a famous opera soprano — is taken hostage at a diplomatic dinner party in South America. The virtuoso novel that deservedly put Patchett on the literary map.

Nevil Shute, *A Town Like Alice*
Best known as a BBC miniseries, Shute's compelling war romance tells the story of a young woman who survives a Japanese death march in World War II and returns to England, only to be drawn back to the Malayan villagers who helped her and the Australian soldier who risked his life to save the former prisoners.

Elizabeth Strout, *Olive Kitteridge*
A "novel in stories," largely centered on the character of Olive Kitteridge, a retired schoolteacher in the small town of Crosby, Maine. At times instinctively wise about her fellow citizens but blind to her own flaws and needs, Olive is a deeply realized protagonist readers sometimes love, sometimes hate, but always recognize. Winner of the Pulitzer Prize.

William Styron, *Sophie's Choice*
Styron's towering novel of the Holocaust, interwoven with autobiographical threads of a young Southern writer's coming of age in New York and the passionate but desperate love affair between Sophie, a tormented Polish concentration camp survivor, and Nathan, the mercurial Brooklyn Jew who would save her from the terrible secret of her past.

Tom Wolfe, *The Bonfire of the Vanities*
Known for his searing, satirical send-ups of the '60s, here Wolfe takes on 1980s New York with a sprawling yet incisive portrait of class warfare — corruption, privilege, power, and their opposites. A single scene of an accident in the South Bronx has become indelibly etched in modern urban mythology.

David Wroblewski, *The Story of Edgar Sawtelle*
An extraordinary debut novel that boldly takes on Shakespeare's Hamlet in the person of Edgar, born on a Wisconsin farm, mute and only able to communicate with humans by sign, but with

an innate ability to communicate with the special Sawtelle dogs his family has meticulously bred for generations. When tragedy and betrayal are visited upon Edgar, he learns the true power of language and love.

Markus Zusak, *The Book Thief*
Originally marketed as a young adult novel, this unusual tale set in 1939 Nazi Germany has charmed teenage readers and adults alike. Liesel is a nine-year-old foster child who craves — and steals — books. Set against the grim backdrop of World War II, Leisel, her accordion-playing foster father, her young friend Rudy, and the Jewish fugitive the family hides in the basement all turn to Liesel's books to survive the extraordinary circumstances that bring them together.

And every bit as engaging as any literary fiction — *The Poems of Elizabeth Bishop*. These exactingly crafted poems trace the arc of Bishop's life and brilliant powers of perception, from an orphaned childhood in Massachusetts and Nova Scotia, to her relocation to Petrópolis, Brazil, to share her life with the fiery architect Lota de Macedo Soares, to her final years in New York City, where Bishop, acknowledged as one of America's finest modern poets, tragically found herself alone and slipping into alcoholism.

on the menu

ASIAN NOODLES WITH SHRIMP

From all these trees,
in the salads, the soup, everywhere,
cherry blossoms fall.

—Basho

Noodles are about the most fun you can have with food. Whether they are eggy flat noodles tossed with butter and parsley, long ribbons of linguine in Alfredo sauce, spun forkfuls of spaghetti in a rich tomato sauce, translucent cellophane shreds, or curly Chinese noodles in savory miso broth, everybody loves noodles. Except Miss Noonan, my fourth-grade teacher — Irish to the core and a stern dispenser of incontrovertible opinion — who insisted that *dough is to bake*, not to boil. Don't tell Italy. In any event, noodles — hot or cold, mixed with an almost infinite choice of sauces, dressings, and additional ingredients — are to my mind, one of civilization's happier discoveries.

It is believed that Marco Polo first encountered noodles in the Chinese court of Kublai Khan around 1295 and brought them to Italy. Others report on what we now call "pasta" being consumed in Italy some decades before that. I'm just glad someone figured out how to knead and roll, pinch and cut, shred and extrude floury dough into ribbons and strands we can boil up in minutes for a satisfying feast.

This dish is one of my favorites to serve in warm weather. It can be made early on the day of your book club meeting and chilled till an hour or so before you are ready to serve it. It's beautiful to look at: light, healthful, and consumed, of course, with a pair of chopsticks in hand — a source of  entertainment in its own right. It is also a preparation ripe for improvisation and using up what's on hand. Chicken or cooked fish can substitute for shrimp. Tinned Asian water chestnuts, bamboo shoots, or baby corn rinsed well in cold water and tossed dry can also fill in for some fresh vegetables. Garnish the finished bowl with a few hard-boiled eggs, or add extra shredded cabbage and noodles to the base to stretch the dish for unexpected guests. You can also divide the base of cabbage and noodles into two large platters and embellish each with different elements — shrimp and Asian vegetables in one, chicken, celery, sweet peppers, and crushed nuts in the other. It's also delicious as leftovers, though with a large group, I'm rarely left with any — someone always makes that last dive with the chopsticks.

Make your dressing in advance, and let the flavors meld together at room temperature. Most of the light ingredients here — noodles, cabbage, white vegetables — have a mild taste and need to absorb the piquant *umami* of the dressing, which is what really makes this dish. So taste your mixture several times, and be sure you are happy with the final flavor.

• ASIAN NOODLES WITH SHRIMP AND VEGETABLES •

1 small head Chinese cabbage, chopped into $^1/_4$" shreds

1 lb. curly or buckwheat (soba) Asian noodles

1 cup sugar snap peas, rinsed in cold water and sliced in half lengthwise

1 red pepper, sliced in thin strips about 2" long

1 cup shredded carrot or daikon radish

4 crisp, outer celery stalks, cut into thin slices on the diagonal (This is, of course, a visual flourish, but one I think is worth bothering with when making an Asian dish.)

1 medium cucumber, seeded and chopped to a medium dice

1 lb. cooked and cleaned medium or small salad shrimp

Chopped peanuts or toasted sesame seeds, for garnish (optional)

For the dressing:

1 tbsp. finely chopped scallion

1 tsp. minced fresh ginger

1 tbsp. Dijon mustard

1 tsp. honey

2 tbsp. tamari sauce

2 tbsp. fresh lemon juice

1 tbsp. rice vinegar

$^1/_2$ cup light olive oil

2 tsp. sesame oil

Serves 6

Dressing: Whisk the first seven ingredients together until well blended. Slowly whisk in olive oil in a thin stream until emulsified. Whisk in sesame oil by droplets. Set aside.

Preparation: Place the shredded cabbage in the bottom of a large serving bowl, such as a pasta platter. Boil the noodles according to the directions, then drain and toss with a few drops of oil to prevent sticking. Spread the hot noodles on top of the cabbage in the serving bowl. Over the hot noodles, scatter the snap peas, pepper strips, shredded carrot, and celery slices. Pour the dressing over the layers and top with the diced cucumber and shrimp. May be chilled for several hours. Allow to come to nearly room temperature before serving. If you are not worried about allergies, a sprinkling of chopped peanuts is a nice finish. Alternatively, try a scattering of toasted sesame seeds.

Your book group might like to nibble on tamari rice crackers, edamame, or lo mein noodles before the meal. The main dish needs no accompaniments, but some fresh pineapple chunks or cherries are a nice, clean finish to this flavorful meal. And I'm always a fan of fortune cookies — everyone likes fortune cookies.

JULY / SUMMER MYSTERIES

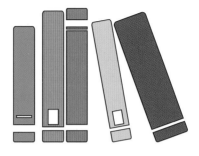

There's the scarlet thread of murder running through
the colorless skein of life, and our duty is to unravel it,
and isolate it, and expose every inch of it.

–Sir Arthur Conan Doyle, *A Study in Scarlet*

I HAVE A weakness for murder mysteries. I blame it on Carolyn
Keene, the apocryphal author of the Nancy Drew series of detective
novels for girls. Carolyn Keene was, of course, a syndicate of
assorted writers who cranked out the formulaic sleuthing plots of
Nancy, her eternally noncommittal "beau," Ned, curious gal-pals
Bess and George, her wise and widowed father, Carson Drew, Esq.,
and Hannah Gruen, their long-suffering housekeeper. I'm not sure
what preteens would make of this nonnuclear family cum BFFs
today, but in the unenlightened early 1960s, I, along with millions
of other young girls, accepted them at face value, was tone-deaf
to their clunky, melodramatic dialogue, and, on lazy summer days,
could happily tear through several volumes.

To me, there is still nothing quite so delicious as losing yourself
in a well-wrought murder mystery. Weaving your way through a

labyrinth of twists, turns, hot leads, and dead ends, you know it will all get solved in the end. The victims will be avenged, and the murderer will be hunted down and dealt his just rewards. What head scratching you might do is involuntary. Mostly you sip your lemonade, follow along, and let your hard-working sleuths run around and wear themselves out. Meanwhile, your own world with all its duties, headaches, and deadlines simply evaporates for a few hours. A good mystery can be a kind of mini vacation from your life.

I don't know if the British actually write better murder mysteries than anyone else, or a whole lot of us just like reading them more. It is probably the latter — something about skullduggery and mayhem lurking just beneath the gleaming surface of a properly run English manor house, complete with starchy, uniformed servants, tea times, foxhounds, and bejeweled dinner guests. We get to slip in the side door of these opulent estates, uncover dark deeds among the upper crust, and watch in delight as a Miss Marple or Detective Poirot tosses a pail of cold water onto all that faux propriety and self-regard. American detectives might have come closest to this kind of class deflation with television's wonderfully disheveled Detective Columbo, who was forever taking down Hollywood starlets, industrial titans, or political poseurs just when they thought they had gotten away with murder. Of course, there is no national monopoly on great English-language mystery novels. American writers, from Poe to Dashiell Hammett, Raymond Chandler, and Sue Grafton, have carved out their own places of honor in the canon. Mary Higgins Clark, Tony Hillerman, Gregory Mcdonald, Robert B. Parker, and Elizabeth George (an American author who sets her popular Inspector Lynley series in Great Britain) consistently top readers' lists of favorites. Native New Zealander Dame Edith Ngaio Marsh claims fans worldwide for her Inspector

Roderick Alleyn mysteries, and Canadian writer Louise Penny, creator of the beloved Chief Inspector Gamache series, has penned no fewer than ten award-winning murder mysteries set in the deceptively tranquil village of Three Pines, south of Montreal.

A growing number of recent films and TV dramas, including some brilliantly conceived, acted, and directed shows, now spare us nothing in the realm of graphic violence and gore. Consequently, many of us find it a relief to retreat to the pages of an old-fashioned whodunit known in the book business as "cozy mysteries." You can find cozy mysteries and mystery series woven around almost any theme: politicians plotting evil, mayhem in the military, foul goings-on in the world of sports, backstabbing in Hollywood, and desperate dealings in the art world. There are medical mysteries with physician sleuths, canny clergy members, and lawyer snoops. There are chefs and sous-chefs unraveling kitchen conundrums, and literary puzzles that can only be solved by authors or bookstore owners.

Not long ago, I discovered the wonderful literary mysteries of the Irish novelist Tana French: *In the Woods* and its sequel, *The Likeness*, followed by *Faithful Place*, *Broken Harbor*, and her latest, *The Secret Place*. She is the kind of writer who lures me in, hook, line, and sinker. It's dangerous to start a Tana French novel. Immersed in her world of quick and quirky police detectives and troubled but deeply human suspects, victims, and witnesses, you

barely come up for food or sleep. The same goes for her British contemporary Kate Atkinson, who crafts seductive literary mysteries with lush descriptions of family life and distinctively British turns of phrase. Her intricate plot turns, complex characters, and underlying social conscience make for unusually intelligent whodunits.

july reads

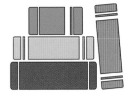

Here is a list of mystery novels, old and new, that enrich the genre. Some aspire to great literature, and some are police procedurals or conventionally plotted murder mysteries. But all provide that heady transport into a world of good and evil, where wits are pitted against the clock and, most happily, none of the urgency is our own.

Kate Atkinson, *Case Histories*
Debut novel by one of the best of the new breed of "literary" crime writers. Private eye and former detective Jackson Brodie goes back 30 years to unravel three interwoven crimes centered on an eccentric British family of sisters.

Agatha Christie, *And Then There Were None*
Ten strangers, each harboring a dark secret, are lured to the remote Indian Island by a mysterious host, where they begin to get killed off one by one. Formerly titled *Ten Little Indians*, this is one of Christie's most brilliant and baffling mysteries.

Daphne du Maurier, *Rebecca*
"Last night I dreamt I went to Manderley again" opens Du Maurier's gothic romance. When a British woman marries a widower with an impressive country estate in Cornwall, she is pitted against its overbearing housekeeper, Mrs. Danvers, who is devoted to the late mistress of the estate, Rebecca.

Ken Follett, *Eye of the Needle*
Ken Follett's 1978 spy thriller, set in the ending days of World War II. A mysterious secret agent and a lonely Englishwoman living on a remote island square off against a ruthless assassin who holds the key to a Nazi victory. Lauded for its taut, detailed plot turns and edge-of-your-seat suspense, this page-turner is one of Follett's most celebrated titles.

Tana French, *In the Woods*
French's impressive debut novel, in which a child who witnessed an unsolved mystery in a quiet Dublin suburb finds himself investigating a chillingly similar murder 20 years later. This richly woven tale established the Irish author as a writer of utterly engrossing and lyrically crafted suspense fiction that holds readers in its grip up to the final page.

Tana French, *Likeness*
In this first-rate follow-up to *In the Woods*, French reintroduces Detective Cassie Maddox, who is called to investigate the murder of a woman who is virtually her twin. When Cassie's ID from a previous alias is discovered on the victim, she goes undercover in a house full of graduate students at Trinity College to solve the murder of her doppelgänger.

Sue Grafton, *A Is for Alibi*
The first book in the alphabet series, featuring Detective Kinsey Millhone, a new breed of sassy-smart, resourceful, and flawed female investigator. Grafton is credited with modernizing the genre with this beloved mystery series.

Dashiell Hammett, *The Maltese Falcon*
The best known of Hammett's Sam Spade detective novels, due in large part to Humphrey Bogart's portrayal in the noir film version. When his partner is killed on a stakeout, Spade must clear himself from suspicion. The cunning plot includes ruthless villains, a gorgeous but elusive redhead, and a priceless gold statuette of a falcon that everyone is desperate to find. The originator of the hard-boiled private eye, Hammett is considered the master of the genre.

Thomas Harris, *Red Dragon*
The psychological thriller that predated Harris's blockbuster *The Silence of the Lambs*, introducing Hannibal Lecter and the FBI agent who tracked him down. A richly imagined psychological

thriller that probes the dark psychosis of a serial killer, told with heart-pounding urgency.

Louise Penny, *Still Life*

Penny's first novel of ten in her best-selling and surprisingly nuanced mystery series featuring Chief Inspector Gamache of the Sûreté du Québec. Beneath the seemingly tranquil surface of the small village of Three Pines lurk dark secrets and surprising human motivations, which Gamache struggles to unravel. Winner of many prestigious awards for the genre, Penny's series is admired for its subtleties and nuanced explorations of human nature.

Alice Sebold, *The Lovely Bones*

A genre-defying coming-of-age story, narrated from heaven by the teenage victim of a brutal murderer, as she looks down on her grieving family and friends — her killer still at large — and the police detective at a loss to solve the case. An unusual and affecting novel of love, loss, and human survival that put Sebold on best-seller lists around the world.

Donna Tartt, *The Goldfinch*

When 13-year-old Theo loses his mother in a violent New York City incident, he is suddenly uprooted and ricocheted between a friend's wealthy Park Avenue family, his estranged father in Las Vegas, a mysterious Greenwich Village antiques shop and its big-hearted proprietor, and beyond. At the center of this expansive novel is a mystery surrounding a small and priceless painting, which drags Theo into the global art underworld. Densely plotted and rich with memorable characters, drama, and human passions, *The Goldfinch* earned Tartt the 2014 Pulitzer Prize.

on the menu

EASY MACARONI SALAD WITH SUMMER CORN AND VEGETABLES

After violent emotion, most people
and all boys demand food.

–Rudyard Kipling, *Captains Courageous*

When I was nine years old, I went to sleepaway summer camp
in Maine for eight weeks. Some of today's young parents might
consider this tantamount to child abuse, but I adored camp.
I'm told that on my first camp drop-off day, my mother found
me sitting on the camp office steps, blithely chatting with some
counselors. When it was time for her to leave, I waved her off
without a sniffle. Since she had gone to the same camp as a girl,
and had extolled its wonders to me for years, she was doubtless
relieved and not really surprised. Though, looking back now, I
am a bit surprised. I was generally a shy child in new situations
and quite attached to my mother. But somehow, homesickness
never entered the camp picture. I loved everything about it: the
piney-scented woods, the activities, the people, I loved the *food*.
Everyone did.

Summoned to our meals by a familiar schedule of bugle calls
and dinner bells, we assembled hungrily outside the dining hall
three times a day. Rain or shine, breakfasts were alternating eggs
(hard-boiled, fried, or fluffy faux scrambled), and on nonegg days,
pancakes or French toast. Once every other Sunday, our tireless

cooks got up at some god-awful hour and made a delicacy known as "wild donuts": pinches of sweet dough, hand dropped in a deep fryer and dusted in sugar. These hot little fritterlike donuts were then torn into bits with our fingers and drowned in maple syrup, to be chased around the plate with one's fork and gobbled. They were everyone's favorite, and extras were raffled off like lottery tickets.

Camp lunches were hot and hearty: corned beef and cabbage, beef stew with flaky baking-powder biscuits, and, every Friday, baked white fish topped with cornflakes, which gave it a curious but not unpleasant sweet taste, simultaneously crunch and soggy.

On it went: a predictable, pleasing rotation of hearty, plain food we anticipated knowingly and consumed voraciously. Young and growing, and running nonstop from one activity to another, I suppose we were quite simply very hungry. Bird pellets might have tasted good to us. But those unchanging, well-remembered meals, reliably served by devoted and resourceful chefs, provided comfort and pleasure.

A lifetime of summers and summer meals later, our taste buds evolve, but some of the simplest foods, eaten with good companions in the warm summer air, still deliver the sunniest memories. One summer I visited dear friends in their wonderful country home in the mountains of upstate New York bringing with me a basket of summer vegetables from our local farmers' market in Maine. She is a former coworker and does not cook. Or need to. He is a French Master Chef, brought up through the French apprentice system, and as natural a cook as you will ever find. Over decades of visits, he has served me some of the most delectable fine cuisine I have ever eaten.

When lunchtime rolled around, he announced that we would go for a picnic by the river. From his stocked refrigerator, he retrieved a Ziploc bag of plain, cooked elbow macaroni and another bag containing several ears of corn on the cob left over from the night before. He proceeded to cut the kernels from the cob, and both the macaroni and corn went into a large plastic container. Dipping into the Maine produce, he sliced and diced radishes, sweet peppers, chives, fresh basil, and herbs; quartered the large cherry tomatoes; and tumbled it all in together. Over this mixture went a generous pour of olive oil, a shake of balsamic vinegar, a dash of his own homemade red wine vinegar, a pinch of sea salt, several grinds of black pepper, and some freshly grated Parmesan cheese. Our simple pasta salad with bread and hard-boiled eggs was as delectable as any gourmet feast he had ever prepared for us. If I used to belittle the humdrum macaroni salad (which I did), I do so no longer. Using decent pasta and compatible, fresh ingredients lightly dressed (please, no mayonnaise), it is endlessly versatile and can showcase summer's bounty with the best of them.

• EASY MACARONI SALAD •

1 lb. good-quality elbow macaroni or other small pasta, cooked and cooled
3 ears cooked corn on the cob, kernels pared off
6–8 radishes, sliced
2 pickling cukes, mostly peeled and chopped in small pieces
2 cups firm cherry tomatoes, halved or quartered
1 medium yellow pepper or mild green pepper, such as Cubanelle,
    chopped
$1/2$ cup fresh basil leaves, torn in small pieces
2 tbsp. fresh chives
2 tbsp. capers
$1/2$ cup crumbled goat cheese

For the dressing:
$1/2$ cup extra-virgin olive oil
1 tbsp. balsamic vinegar
2 tbsp. red wine vinegar
Salt and pepper, to taste

Whole basil sprigs, for garnish
Serves 6

Preparation: Put all ingredients into a large bowl. Pour the olive oil
and vinegars over all and toss lightly to coat. Season with salt and
pepper, to taste. Garnish with whole basil sprigs. Store the salad
chilled for several hours.

It's July. What this summer supper wants to come next is an ice
cream sandwich. Be clever and make your own, or just hit your
grocer's freezer.

AUGUST/CLOUD DRIFTING

The house was quiet and the world was calm.
The reader became the book; and summer night
Was like the conscious being of the book. . . .

–Wallace Stevens, excerpted from the poem
"The House Was Quiet and the World Was Calm,"
from *Harmonium*

I HAVE ALWAYS loved August. I love everything about the month —
the sound of the word, the elegant look of its letters, its full 31 days
of summer, its leggy wildflowers, and its long afternoons and warm
nights on the porch with a good book. Absent the hysteria of high
summer's requisite road trips, visits, beaching, boating, camps, and
cookouts, August slows to a lovely pace. You can watch the sky.

I confess to a certain prejudice, since it's my birthday month. As
a child, I always felt smugly advantaged to be out of school and
able to host my birthday party at the beach or neighborhood pool
as one final holiday — a last hurrah before Labor Day.

Birthdays as adults are tricky business. We think we would like to
ignore them, but anyone who has had the unhappy experience of

having a birthday go by, completely forgotten or ignored, knows that it leaves you inexplicably bereft. No matter how old you are. Fortunately, childhood holds no such paradox. If you were lucky and born to a loving family willing to indulge you, it's a day to pull out the stops, and most of us have, at some juncture, tried to swing for the fences on our birthday. My mother was a traditionalist. She subscribed enthusiastically to traditions, including some that she had never been part of or that predated her by centuries. Many of these notions came from the books and artwork of the quaint New England watercolor illustrator Tasha Tudor, who was herself obsessed with venerating bygone days and the old-fashioned holiday customs of our forebears. When Tudor's illustrated books were readily in print, we often gave one to my mother for her birthday or for Christmas.

One of Tudor's classics was called *Becky's Birthday*. Lavishly illustrated with idyllic summer scenes, it is the story of Becky's tenth birthday, when she begins to feel very grown up, braiding her own hair for the first time, going to the general store by herself, and helping to churn peach ice cream. In the evening, Becky's indefatigable family packs up all sorts of delicious picnic foods in hampers and heads to the river for her birthday supper. In the big finale that charmed its readers, Becky's lighted birthday cake is floated down the currents on a raft to the breathless birthday girl. When I was about the same age, I read and reread *Becky's Birthday*, pondering if there was any remote way my family might be badgered into this kind of Busby Berkeley production for my own birthday. But even at that age, I grasped the difference between reality and some author's runaway sense of vicarious nostalgia.

In the world of children's books, Tudor's fanciful if exhausting reveries of domestic life in simpler times set her and her homespun families in a category by themselves. Her well-written stories and beguiling illustrations were theoretically created for children, but primarily charmed adults. They engendered a kind of wistfulness in her loyal readers, who secretly knew better. While you can smell the fir boughs, apples baking, clove pomanders, and cinnamon buns whipped up for Christmas morning in Tudor's books, you can also get a strong whiff of the dust, cinders, draughts, scratching critters, and dank wood, if you know anything about the old houses of the period she favored. Even her most devoted followers realized that churning butter and storing it in the brook-fed icehouse could not possibly be all that much fun. As Tudor's real children grew up, stories of familial dysfunction started to leak out. Tudor could wreak havoc by making her kids dress up in antique costumes to serve as her models, and by having them reenact laborious chores like hand laundry or candle making, long since abandoned as necessities of American life. But there is no denying the artistry and charm of her considerable opus. It garnered her a generation of devoted readers who found great pleasure in dropping back a century into a slower, gentler world — including my mother and, for a brief series of long-ago Augusts, me.

Many book and writing groups take summer months off, but I advise against it. They are the loveliest months for informal, relaxed gatherings, and many temporarily disbanded clubs will attest that their good practice, disrupted in summer, can be hard to rekindle in September. I say don't assign a book. Let everyone read what he or she has been craving to crack open all year, and then have each member give a little précis, a thumbs-up or -down. After all, these are readers whose tastes and enthusiasms you know. Where better to find perfect book recommendations or to be warned against wasting time on a dud? August is high summer, and summer is all about pleasure — lost hours and private vacations of the mind.

august reads

For book club members who don't already have an August
title in mind, here are some popular choices recommended by those who
favor the chaise longue and the beach chair. Some are guaranteed page-
turners. Others lend themselves to short stints of reading — you can pick
them up and put them down again between swims or naps in the hammock.

John Berendt, *Midnight in the Garden of Good and Evil*
Originally conceived as a piece of high-society investigative
journalism for *Esquire* magazine, *Midnight* is a modern-day crime
story set in Savannah, and is the basis for the acclaimed movie by
the same title, starring Kevin Spacey.

John Cheever, *The Stories of John Cheever*
Winner of the 1979 Pulitzer Prize, and now a classic of the
genre. Cheever's masterful short stories of suburban ennui in
the affluent Northeast are full of shady green lawns, commuter
trains, cocktail hours, and the shadows hiding behind the
facades of post–World War II American life. Impeccable craft
distinguishes these extraordinary and often heartbreaking
modern classics of short fiction.

Fannie Flagg, *Fried Green Tomatoes at the Whistle Stop Cafe*
The popular comedienne's warmhearted and folksy Southern
novel of Mrs. Threadgoode, an elderly nursing home resident,
and her loyal visitor, Evelyn, who is struggling through the
doldrums of middle age. As Mrs. Threadgoode shares with
Evelyn the story of her young life growing up in Whistle Stop,
Alabama, the bond between the two women deepens, leading to
the novel's wonderfully satisfying and affecting conclusion. Flagg
distinguishes herself as a wise and lovable storyteller in the best
Southern tradition.

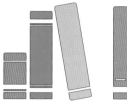

Julia Glass, *Three Junes*

A remarkable debut novel that follows the life of a Scottish family over a decade and around the globe, from the Greek islands to their ancestral home in rural Scotland, and to New York's Greenwich Village and the Hamptons, in three interconnected stories all taking place in June of different years. A fearless and unforgettable novel about what it means to be part of a family.

Arthur Golden, *Memoirs of a Geisha*

This runaway best-seller lifts the curtain on the mysterious and secretive world of geisha artisans and courtesans. It follows the life of one of Japan's most celebrated geishas, from her humble fishing village to the highest circles of society and influence. Exotic, intriguing, and totally unforgettable.

Laura Hillenbrand, *Seabiscuit*

One of the great American underdog sagas: the true story of Seabiscuit, a bargain-basement-priced racehorse with crooked legs and a heart as big as the country he won over, and the unlikely trio of owner-trainer-jockey who made him an American icon in the 1930s.

John Irving, *A Prayer for Owen Meany*

Irving's beloved 1989 novel of friendship and fate, with a dose of mysticism thrown in. Dwarfish Owen Meany, a stonecutter's son, has accidentally killed the young narrator's mother with a misdirected baseball. Meany, who speaks in a high-pitched (ALL CAPS) voice, becomes convinced that he can only be redeemed by an act of great martyrdom. Wholly original and completely engrossing, this is Irving at his creative best.

Colleen McCullough, *The Thorn Birds*

Three generations of passion, ambition, betrayal, and forbidden love on the Australian outback, from 1915 to post–World War II. McCullough's saga of a young priest entangled with a powerful matriarch and her family became a landmark television miniseries watched by millions around the globe.

Larry McMurtry, *Lonesome Dove*

The Pulitzer Prize–winning Western drama of two former Texas Rangers turned cattle rustlers, as they embark on an epic cattle drive from the sleepy town of Lonesome Dove, Texas, to Montana. The extraordinary lead and secondary characters in this engrossing story of settling the frontier wilderness have earned it a devoted following and qualify it as a classic novel of the American West.

Helen Simonson, *Major Pettigrew's Last Stand*

A brother's death spurs a retired British major and traditional aristocratic gentleman to befriend a Pakistani widow and local shopkeeper, much to the shock of his neighbors and family. The two discover how much they have in common, despite the constraints of traditional English country life, in this utterly charming novel.

Virginia Woolf, *To the Lighthouse*

Woolf's enigmatic novel of interior lives, explored through the experiences of the affluent Ramsay family between 1910 and 1920, and centered on their holiday to the Isle of Skye.

And if you want to go back and read Nancy Drew or a stack of classic comic books, that would be okay too. It's August.

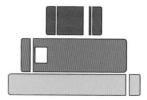

on the menu

GREEK SHRIMP AND RICE SALAD

. . . Aesop left a legacy of poetry while cooking as a slave.

—Theresa Karas Yianilos, *The Complete Greek Cookbook*

Alfresco: in cool air. As in, dining alfresco. It seems that when people around the world — especially those who, by choice or by strife, have been displaced and transplanted away from their home — speak or write of their best memory of family and the life they left behind, they invariably conjure up some version of what Americans think of as a backyard family picnic. It is the ultimate idyll: sitting out of doors in fine weather, with family and friends, eating and drinking simple foods that have been lovingly made, there is a profound ease and comfort to these casual, pastoral gatherings. They imprint themselves on our memories with special joy. No surprise that pictures of open-air dining are probably the most common promotional images in the travel industry, second only to suntanned vacationers swimming in azure waters.

I myself subscribe to moving lunches, cocktails, dinners, and even breakfasts outside to the deck as soon as it can be considered remotely feasible. Living in the Northeast, we have a short but glorious season for such pleasures. I am not above exhorting my husband to bundle up in a parka to begin the alfresco season, tipping our face up into pale March sun and imagining the long days of high summer ahead. Back in the early '70s, when my family lived in a small town on the Merrimack River north of Boston, the old Victorian house next door to us went up for sale. We peeked furtively out our windows at the real estate agents ushering assorted prospects around the property, fretting about our potential new neighbors. Eventually the house was bought by a young Greek American couple, still in their 20s. She was an artist and Pre-Raphaelite beauty from Connecticut. He had been born on the Greek island of Crete and was dark, handsome, compact, and bristling with purposeful energy. Within weeks of their arrival, it was apparent that our ho-hum New England life was about to be turned on its ear. Our new neighbors wasted no time getting down to work on what would become a sprawling, Mediterranean-style farm — a voluptuous spread of free-form flower and vegetable gardens, and terra-cotta pots of fragrant herbs everywhere. The ramshackle barn was shored up and filled with livestock — horses, goats, a donkey once, and assorted ducks and geese. They set up beehives, harvesting and bottling the honey. They named it Seven Acre Farm and would, in time, raise three children there in our tidy and conventional little town. They were exactly what it needed.

In celebration of their Greek heritage, they filled their home with woven shawls and pillows in the bright colors of the Aegean. Their original artwork, photos, and paintings covered the walls. Free-spirited, huge-hearted, creative, incredibly hardworking, and endlessly attentive and generous to us, our new neighbors became our extended and much-beloved family.

On my days off from some mind-numbing summer job waiting on tables or answering phones, my mother, sister, and I often wandered across the yard in the late afternoon, with a bottle of champagne, to sit with our neighbors under their grape arbor. Sprawled in old lawn chairs, we'd sip the afternoon away, reveling in their stories of life in

Greece and their young romance in the islands. As the kids came around, hungry for dinner, platters of mezes would appear on the big picnic table, followed by salads, grilled meats, and stuffed vegetables. In the best, long days of summer, we sat out late, drinking wine with soft cheese and fruits or honey-saturated sweets. Heady with good food and wine, I could easily imagine myself at a sidewalk café by the Aegean, quaffing ouzo under the warm summer stars. When I finally did get to the Greek isles some years later, it felt like home.

It was from these shared meals around our neighbors' welcoming table that I first became enthralled with Greek- and Mediterranean-style cookery — a cuisine totally new to many of us in the early '70s. They introduced our tame New England palates to such exotic provender as olive oil, feta cheese, thick strained yogurt, fresh basil, and imported olives — staples I now could not live without. They showed us how to feed ourselves from the garden and the land, to eat what each season presents. The timing of this education coincided with the country's burgeoning "natural" foods movement, led by young people living on farm cooperatives and communes. New scrutiny of preservatives in food, concern over pesticides and food-borne illness, and interest in healthy eating for disease prevention swept the national consciousness. Experts did not yet speak about the Mediterranean diet, and we had not yet coined the term "locavore," but the American food revolution was underway. For me, it all started with watching, learning, and sharing delicious, homegrown food on those summer evenings with friends and family — a gastronomic coming of age at the picnic table.

The dish on the following page is not an authentic Greek preparation, but my own creation in the spirit of those spontaneous summer picnics. It is great for a group, gets raves from everyone, and can be made ahead and chilled until you are ready to serve it.

· GREEK SHRIMP AND RICE SALAD ·

5 cups cooked white rice, cooled to room temperature (should be
    cooked with several tablespoons of olive oil to keep the grains from
    sticking together)
3 scallions, finely chopped
1 cup frozen petite peas, thawed
⅔ cup pitted and chopped Kalamata olives
2 medium cucumbers, mostly peeled, seeded and diced
1 green pepper, diced
2 cups firm cherry tomatoes, quartered
¼ cup leaf parsley, chopped
1 tbsp. fresh or 1 tsp. dried dill
2 tsp. dried oregano, or 2 tbsp. fresh oregano
⅔ cup crumbled feta cheese
1 lb. small shrimp, cooked and chilled
Green leaf lettuce or other large lettuce leaves
Fresh basil, for garnish

For the dressing:
¼ cup fresh lemon juice
1 tbsp. good wine vinegar
1 tsp. sea salt
¾ cup olive oil
Freshly ground pepper

Serves 6

Dressing: Whisk the lemon juice, vinegar, and sea salt together until foamy. Slowly pour in olive oil in a fine stream, whisking to emulsify. Add a few grinds of pepper and whisk in. Set aside.

Preparation: Put the cooked rice in a large mixing bowl and stir to separate the grains. Add in prepared scallions, peas, olives, cucumbers, green pepper, and tomatoes and fold together. Sprinkle with parsley, dill, oregano, and feta cheese. Pour the dressing over the rice mixture and stir gently to blend. Carefully fold in the shrimp. Line a large serving bowl with green leaf or other large lettuce leaves, well washed and stemmed. Spoon the rice salad over the lettuce and garnish with fresh basil.

Note: If the salad is made ahead, chill covered and do not add shrimp until just before serving, as the acidic dressing will break down the shrimp. I think this dish is best served just slightly chilled — almost room temperature.

If you would like a little more going on with this meal, you can arrange the salad on a deep platter and surround it with a ring of fresh green beans sprinkled with lemon juice. Either way, this is a wonderful summer meal, especially when served with warm pita bread. Put out a plate of chilled watermelon slices for the evening book discussion. Your book group will be glad it didn't take a summer recess. *Gia'sou!*

SEPTEMBER / TIME TRAVEL

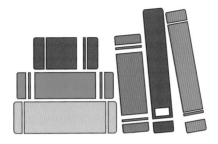

The past is really almost as much a work
of the imagination as the future.

–Jessamyn West

I CAN'T BE sure, but I believe the first work of historical fiction
I ever read was *Lorna Doone: A Romance of Exmoor* by Richard
Doddridge Blackmore, a writer whose name few would now
recognize — possibly with good reason. The novel's labyrinthine
plot of clan battles and kidnappings in the 17th-century Highlands
is now lost to me. The best part of the novel may be the eponymous
heroine's name, which survives as a square Nabisco shortbread
cookie. But I do remember the sensation of peering down that long
telescope of time into a lost past — foreign, florid, and faraway.
And for the duration of those days that I slogged through Lorna
Doone's trials and triumphs, I know I still preferred those dreamy,
suspended hours of time travel to the unspectacular routines of my
own middle school life.

I had a sixth-grade teacher who was a fiend for Dickens. We
read *Great Expectations* and *Oliver Twist*. The Victorian verbosity

took some getting used to, but many of us ended up engrossed in both the stories and the unique wit that delivered them. We also soldiered through Dumas' *The Three Musketeers* and *The Count of Monte Cristo*. Some great works, such as Cervantes's *Don Quixote*, were considered too ambitious for us, so they were presented in abridged form as part of a "Classics Reader" series.

In junior high, we passed around copies of James A. Michener's *Hawaii* and *Tales of the South Pacific*; T. H. White's *The Once and Future King*, and Leon Uris's weighty and engrossing *Exodus*. I had a brief love affair with the rigors of pioneer life in the American West with Willa Cather's *My Ántonia*. There were times when the books I read seemed adult beyond my years. And there were periods when I seemed to be reverting to books written for younger readers. But, with a middle school teacher for a mother, no one in our household bothered to make much distinction between age-appropriate or inappropriate literature. Nor were works of great literature especially promoted over potboilers. If it was on our bookshelves or in the library, it was mine to read.

In some sense, almost all fiction is historical fiction. Simply by setting a story in a realistic and known past, the author has created a piece of historical fiction. In fact, almost every novel that is not futuristic science fiction or fantasy could be considered a historical novel — even if it concerns events of six months ago. Historical fiction always walks that fine line between fact and imagined realities. Its locations, set designs, costumes, and color appear more vivid the farther they are from our own history. But it is the characters and their hypothetical adventures in the past that can enlighten and engage us with history, in ways that purely documentary accounts rarely can.

september reads

The first hints of shortening days seem to demand industry of us. Stepping up our reading selections to exercise drifty summer brains is a good start. Here are some captivating works of historical fiction to consider. They range from literary masterworks to popular fiction, but each, in its way, will leave you enlightened and a bit wiser for having looked back into the long tunnel of history.

Geraldine Brooks, *March*
> The absent father in Louisa May Alcott's classic *Little Women* becomes the focal character in this arresting novel set against the backdrop of the American Civil War. This beautifully written story breathes new life into the March family and shines a light on the impacts of that war on those who fought it and those who waited at home.

Anthony Doerr, *All the Light We Cannot See*
> The forces of history, fate, and love come together in the interwoven stories of a blind young girl and her locksmith father, who flee Paris in 1944, and a German orphan whose talent for building radios makes him a vital recruit to the Hitler Youth. Doerr's prose, daring narrative structure, and breadth of knowledge make this novel a major literary achievement.

Jeff Foltz, *Two Men Ten Suns*
> A work of speculative historical fiction that pits two men — one American, one Japanese — in a deadly contest as their governments push them to be the first to develop a nuclear weapon. Based on extensive research, this previously unexplored scenario is an engrossing and totally plausible addition to the body of World War II literature.

Ben Fountain, *Billy Lynn's Long Halftime Walk*
   A heartrending comic novel of soldiers on leave from the Iraq
   War and the Hollywood PR machine that promises fame and
   hard cash for their story, plus a halftime appearance at a Dallas
   Cowboys game on Thanksgiving Day. A searingly honest and
   affecting novel about modern America's power, privilege, and
   the so-called War on Terror. This novel is destined to become a
   classic in the literature of our current global conflicts.

Charles Frazier, *Cold Mountain*
   In the final days of the Civil War, Inman, a gravely wounded
   Confederate soldier, sets off to walk home to Ada, the woman he
   loves. Meanwhile, Ada struggles to eke out an existence on her
   late father's farm, until she is aided by another young woman,
   the itinerant Ruby, who teaches her how to survive.

David Guterson, *Snow Falling on Cedars*
   A courtroom drama that follows the trial of a Japanese American
   accused in the drowning of a local fisherman off a remote island
   north of Puget Sound. Over the brutal winter of the trial, the island
   and its residents struggle with their haunted history as an American
   internment camp for Japanese Americans during World War II.

Hilary Mantel, *Wolf Hall*
   The acclaimed work of historical fiction that delves deep into the
   complex and brilliant political machinations of Thomas Cromwell
   in the court of King Henry VIII and Anne Boleyn.

Boris Pasternak, *Doctor Zhivago*
   Pasternak's most famous novel, originally banned in the Soviet
   Union and first published in Italy in 1957. Dr. Yuri Zhivago, a poet/
   physician, is caught between factions in the Russian Revolution
   as he tries to find safe refuge for his family in a rural mountain
   dacha, and is torn between duty to his wife, Tonya, and his
   passion for Lara, a beautiful nurse he has fallen in love with.

Lisa See, *Snow Flower and the Secret Fan*

In 19th-century rural China, seven-year-old Lily is paired with her "old same," Snow Flower, in a spiritual friendship that will bond the two for life. As young girls, they share dreams, secrets, and the agony of traditional foot-binding, passing messages back and forth on the folds of a silk fan. A fascinating glimpse into Chinese history, and the role of female friendship, tested by isolation and confronted by power.

Kathryn Stockett, *The Help*

Set in the racially divided Deep South in the summer of 1962, a privileged, white college grad returns home to Jackson, Mississippi, to find herself unsettled by the schism between the lives of the black domestic help and the white families who employ them. When she invites several of the maids to secretly share their life stories for a book she will write, tensions in the town threaten to boil over.

Alice Walker, *The Color Purple*

The story of Celie, sold by her father as chattel to a heartless husband who separates her from her sister, Nettie — the only person on earth who has ever loved her. Celie survives by sheer willpower, until she meets her husband's lover, the confident, seductive Shug Avery, who teaches Celie the redemptive power of love in this fearless, uplifting novel of human triumph.

Baron Wormser, *Teach Us That Peace*

Set in the politically and racially charged summer of 1962 in Baltimore, a coming-of-age story for young Arthur Mermelstein, and one of personal awakening for his schoolteacher mother, Susan. Richly textured and beautifully rendered, poet Wormser's first novel is reminiscent of Philip Roth's *Portnoy's Complaint*, with its quick, incisive humor, wistfulness, and relentless quest for meaning in the chapters of our own recent history.

on the menu

STROMBOLI

You learn pasta by standing next to people who have been making it their whole lives and watching them. It seems simple and that's because it is simple, but, characteristic of all Italian cooking, it's a simplicity you have to learn. My advice: Go there.

–Bill Buford, *Heat*

The first I ever heard of "Stromboli" was in reference to the Roberto Rossellini/Ingrid Bergman art-house movie I vaguely recall seeing in college. Set on the remote volcanic Italian island of that name, the film was politically and historically dense and enigmatic beyond what I, as a 19-year-old college student, could process. It is now known primarily as the creative liaison that brought together Bergman and Rossellini in an affair that scandalized Hollywood and much of Bergman's adoring American audience.

In any event, I put Stromboli out of my mind for a few decades, until my inspired poet friend, Michelle Lewis, made the wonderful savory stuffed bread called Stromboli. It was a hot, crusty bread stuffed with mushrooms, peppers, herbs, and cheeses, and it was delicious. I have since adopted and adapted Michelle's original Stromboli for dozens of gatherings. Among other pleasures, book club meals are great for this kind of cross-pollination of culinary notions. Someone introduces a dish; the rest of you pocket the idea and make it your own for another occasion. I have served Stromboli with a fruit salad for brunch, and with a green salad for a light supper. Whenever I need a light meal that travels well, Stromboli is my go-to. Neighbors returning from vacation or extended travel to an empty fridge are always delighted to find a savory Stromboli awaiting them. If someone is sick or a family needs a meal brought in, Stromboli will not compete with the ubiquitous casseroles. Kids love it; adults love it. You can wrap it in heavy foil, and you don't even need to retrieve your dishware. Stromboli is happy being refrigerated or frozen and reheated. Like a good soup, it's a delicacy with a sturdy constitution.

Stromboli is essentially rolled-out bread or pizza dough, filled with meats and/or vegetables and cheeses. You pull the dough up to enfold the filling, so you have a kind of savory turnover. It is as versatile as pizza, in terms of potential ingredients. Like turnovers, pies, stuffed dumplings, and other dishes that conceal an inner core, Stromboli offers that element of surprise and discovery when you cut into it. Food like that is just fun.

The amount of dough and how thin you roll it will dictate how much filling you can use and still end up with a full but neat Stromboli when it emerges, puffed and gleaming, from the oven. You can divide the dough and make two smaller ones, slicing them into finger-food rounds for an irresistible appetizer (I guarantee it will be the first platter emptied), or make one big, showy Stromboli for four to six people, such as I suggest here. However you elect to present it, the combinations of ingredients are endless. Tradition includes salami, prosciutto, or spiced ham. Otherwise, use fresh, marinated, pickled, or sautéed vegetables, herbs, and condiments, plus various cheeses. If you use prepared fillings like marinated artichokes or grilled peppers, do be sure to drain and dry them well — wet fillings can ooze through the dough during baking and make a soggy bottom crust.

The following combination is savory and lovely to look at. Other vegetarian options are mentioned at the end of the recipe. You can make, bake, and freeze the Stromboli up to a week or two ahead of time if you like. Just thaw and reheat it, lightly wrapped in foil, in a preheated 400°F (200°C) oven for about 15–20 minutes. Or you can refrigerate the cooked Stromboli overnight and heat it just before serving.

Whatever your schedule, Stromboli looks beautiful and tastes delicious. It is always greeted with enthusiasm and disappears down to the last crusty crumb. If you should have any left over, cut it into small squares, reheat, and serve as appetizers or snacks. And don't forget the egg glaze, sesame seeds, and venting cuts for the top — these steps take just seconds, ensure proper cooking, and give your Stromboli a definite professional flair.

· STROMBOLI ·

1 lb. good-quality pizza dough (preferably fresh, not frozen)
½ cup basil pesto
8 slices provolone cheese, cut into strips
1 6-oz. jar roasted red peppers (about 12 slices), well drained, patted
  dry on paper towels, and cut into thin strips
1 6-oz. jar marinated artichokes, well drained and coarsely chopped
2 cups baby spinach leaves
½ cup grated Parmigiano-Reggiano
Sea salt
Freshly ground black pepper
1 large egg, beaten
1–2 tbsp. sesame seeds

Serves 6

Preparation: Preheat oven to 400°F (200°C). Lightly grease a large cookie sheet or line with parchment paper.

Working on a lightly floured surface, roll the pizza dough into an oblong shape, about 9"x13", lifting and stretching the dough with your hands as needed. Try not to tear the dough; patch and smooth any breaks. Spread a thin layer of pesto over the dough, up to about ¾" from the edges. Cover the dough with the sliced provolone in a single layer, again avoiding the edges of the dough. Arrange the red peppers, chopped artichokes, and spinach over the provolone. Sprinkle with the Parmesan-Reggiano and a little salt and fresh pepper; avoid the outer edges of the dough. Working long edge to long edge, pull the dough up over the filling, pinch it closed, and tuck the short ends under. Place it seam side down and pinch any gaps to form a sealed pocket.

Brush the Stromboli lightly with the beaten egg and sprinkle with sesame seeds. Cut four or five 1" vents in the top of the dough. Bake in the middle of the preheated oven about 30–40 minutes, until golden brown. Let cool 10 minutes, slice, and serve.

Other filling options include: blanched broccoli or chard; sautéed mushrooms; sliced tomatoes; red, yellow, or green bell peppers (these I drizzle with olive oil and cook in the microwave for about 1 minute to soften them); thinly sliced or grated zucchini; new potatoes; or a leftover vegetable dish, such as ratatouille, so long as it is fairly dry. You can add your choice of fresh herbs and cheese to complement the filling. Swiss, Gruyère, mozzarella, fontina, cheddar, and soft goat and feta cheeses would all work well; fresh basil leaves, rosemary, or dill will enhance most of these combinations.

I have found that even the highest-quality pizza dough can become dry and crumbly if frozen and thawed. This recipe works best using fresh, cool dough with lots of elasticity.

You can make, bake, and freeze the Stromboli up to a week or two ahead of time if you like. Just thaw and reheat it, lightly wrapped in foil, in a preheated 400 degree oven for about 15–20 minutes. Or you can refrigerate the cooked Stromboli overnight and heat it just before serving.

OCTOBER / A SHIVER IN THE AIR

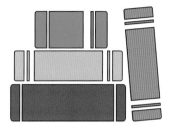

It's what we love the most can make us most afraid . . .

–Pat Schneider, "Going Home the Longest Way Around"

IF YOU EVER went camping as a child, you can probably recall the perverse thrill of tented overnights where someone goads the group into telling crazy ghost stories around the campfire. They have names like "The Golden Arm," "The Man in the Backseat," and "The Changing Tombstone Inscription." All are earnestly sworn to be *true* stories, and every narrator aspires to out-fright the others. Boys and girls love them equally. Surrounded by my best friends and warmed by a cheering fire in the woods, I did too.

Pat Schneider, the wonderful poet and writer from Amherst, Massachusetts, observes in her lovely poem "Going Home the Longest Way Around" how we are all a bit like children wanting to be told scary stories; we are most afraid when what we know, love, and trust the most becomes unrecognizable. The best authors of horror novels know this. They will start us out comfortably, even cozily, in a familiar setting, and then begin, by tiny increments, to move the pieces — or the furniture — around. Small aberrations occur: a glove from a deceased relative appears on the front hall table, a bird is discovered trapped in a room closed up for generations, soft piano music comes wafting from the deserted garden. Something is just slightly wrong. Our protagonist will try to brush it off — just the wind, just my imagination. But we know better, and we're hooked.

I don't recall that I ever intentionally set out to read great amounts of horror fiction, but over the years, I've read more than my share of just mysteries and potboiler beach reads and, I confess to the guilty pleasure of a well-wrought spine-tingler. This does not apply to horror movies, which I simply don't watch. Scaredy-cat that I am, I end up huddled under a blanket with both hands in front of my face, hearing only terrible screams and minor-key soundtracks, so the whole point is lost on me. I do, however, recall that once, during my foreign studies year, I inexplicably accepted a dare from a classmate to accompany him to an all-night horror movie marathon at a London cinema. We watched back-to-back spookiness from midnight to about 6:00 a.m. *The Fall of the House of Usher* is the only film I remember, and I think I slept through most of it. Anything in excess loses its punch.

In putting together my list of recommendations for books in this category, I realize that we run into all kinds of gray area when we try to strictly define horror as its own literary genre. Murder mysteries, tales of the supernatural, novels of magical realism, science fiction, psychological thrillers, and even the well-worn police procedural, when ramped up (think *The Silence of the Lambs*), can all raise goose bumps. There are of course, classics like *Frankenstein* and *Dracula*, and there are inventive modern works, like Gillian Flynn's *Gone Girl*, that build and expand on the genre's conventions. So here I allow a little latitude in what constitutes a horror story — maybe, in homage to the campfire tradition, we will simply call them "scary stories."

october reads

I admit that I do not relish being scared out of my wits or repulsed by gory horror stories. Nevertheless, there is a fair amount of violence and some bloodletting (vampirish and otherwise) on this list. It comes with the territory. These are quite simply some of the great classic horror novels and a few well-done contemporary tales of hauntings, spooks, spirits, and poltergeists that make irresistible reading come the season of goblins.

A. S. Byatt, *Possession*
Two literary critics unearth love letters, journals, and poems that reveal a passionate love affair between an esteemed literary great and a little-known poetess. As they contrive to keep their sensational discovery from fellow researchers, they find themselves drawn into an otherworldly web of intrigue and romance. Winner of England's highest literary award, the Booker Prize.

Charles Dickens, *The Mystery of Edwin Drood*
Edwin Drood is betrothed to the orphan Rosa, but soon after, the engagement is broken off and Edwin disappears. Suspicions of foul play fall upon a typically Dickensian cast of eccentric characters, but here the reader is left to unravel the mystery, since Dickens died during its creation, leaving the famous story unfinished.

Gillian Flynn, *Gone Girl*
Look no further than the black-and-red cover, dense with one- and two-word review bullets: Ingenious, Terrifying, Mercilessly Entertaining, Razor-Sharp, Sinister, Wickedly Clever, Menacing . . . it is all these and more. The story of a young, privileged, and promising couple's marriage gone insanely wrong, this compulsively readable thriller will keep you on the edge of your chair to the final page.

Stephen King, *Misery*

Annie Wilkes is best-selling author Paul Sheldon's most ardent fan. After Sheldon is immobilized in a car accident, she also becomes his nurse and captor, demanding that he write his greatest novel ever — just for her. Trapped in a remote mountain cabin medicated and tortured by Annie, Sheldon travels a dark journey of artistic creation possessed by evil, in this terrifying psycho-thriller with subtle autobiographical insights by the master of modern horror literature.

Gaston Leroux, *The Phantom of the Opera*

A Gothic tale of obsession and ghostly hauntings, set beneath the Paris Opera House. Written a century ago, Leroux's riveting chiller cum romance provided the basis for Andrew Lloyd Webber's Broadway sensation, but the original text offers up lush language, psychological subtleties, and intriguing bits of true history that justify audiences' fascination with the dark tale for over a century.

Carson McCullers, *Reflections in a Golden Eye*

Shocking at the time of its publication in 1941, the life of a Southern army captain and closeted bisexual is upended when he discovers that his outrageously flirtatious wife is having an affair with another officer. Fearless and unflinching, this dark, steamy drama was immortalized by Marlon Brando, Elizabeth Taylor, and John Huston in the 1967 movie.

Toni Morrison, *Beloved*

Based on actual events, Morrison's towering tale of the antebellum South and a runaway slave, who is haunted by the ghostly spirit-presence of her dead two-year-old daughter and memories of Sweet Home, the plantation where unspeakable cruelties defined her life of subjugation. Winner of the Pulitzer Prize, many consider *Beloved* to be Morrison's finest novel — high praise in the context of her impressive body of work.

Edgar Allan Poe, *Edgar Allan Poe: The Complete Tales and Poems*

Well-known and lesser-known masterpieces by the genius creator of "The Tell-Tale Heart," "The Gold-Bug," "The Fall of the House of Usher," and *The Raven*. Chilling, mesmerizing, brilliant work by a tortured soul and one of America's greatest writers in any genre.

Anne Rice, *Interview with the Vampire*

Rice's dazzling reinvention of the vampire myth in which Lestat, a powerful and seductive vampire, tells his story to an unlikely young interviewer. Shockingly erotic and hypnotic, Lestat's confessions reveal profound contemplations on mortality and the nature of evil, as the vampire becomes a sympathetic and all-too-human figure.

Mary Shelley, *Frankenstein*

Shelley's still-frightening 1818 masterpiece, in which she conjures scientific experimentation run amok when a monstrous life is created on the laboratory table. Written when she was just 19, Frankenstein remains one of the greatest horror novels of all time.

Robert Louis Stevenson, *The Strange Case of Dr. Jekyll and Mr. Hyde*

Suffering from sensations of a divided self, Stevenson, a respected doctor by day, dreamed that he walked the dark alleys of Edinburgh by night as a dark alter ego. In 1886, he wrote down the story of his nightmare existence as two men — one good and one evil — who struggled for control of his soul. The book, one of the first to speak of the psychosis of the "split personality," became an overnight sensation.

Donna Tartt, *The Little Friend*

Best-selling author Tartt's second novel set in Alexandria, Mississippi, where one Mother's Day, a little boy named Robin is found hanged from a tree in his family's backyard. Twelve years later, the murder remains unsolved. Robin's spirited younger sister, Harriet, and her worshipful best friend, Hely, set out to discover and punish the killer. Extraordinary characters fill this richly atmospheric novel — at times humorous, heartbreaking, and outright scary.

Sarah Waters, *The Little Stranger*
A once-prominent family struggles to keep up their crumbling Georgian mansion, Hundreds Hall, and their fading way of life in post–World War II Warwickshire, England. When a respectable country doctor — the son of a former parlor maid at the mansion — arrives to attend to a traumatized servant, mysterious events suggest that Hundreds Hall is haunted by more than the changing times. Brushed with the supernatural, this old-fashioned haunted-house story is deftly executed for an engrossing, spine-tingling read.

H. G. Wells, *The Island of Dr. Moreau*
A mad scientist toils in his remote island laboratory to turn animals into humans, with terrifying results. Considered the father of science fiction, Wells weaves grotesque specters of future scientific experimentation into a horror story that has captivated readers for generations.

on the menu

SPANISH CHICKPEAS WITH SPINACH

If you take away from food the wholeness of growing it
or take away the joy and conviviality of preparing
it in your own home, then I believe you are talking
about a whole new definition of the human being.

–Wendell Berry, *The Unsettling of America*

One of the great pleasures of living in or near an energetic city is
the option to dine out at its restaurants. I have the good fortune
to live just outside Portland, Maine, which in 2009 was named
"America's foodiest small town" by *Bon Appétit* magazine. The
honor has continued to attract chefs, restaurateurs, and purveyors
of gourmet foods, and has been great for our local economy. For
us full-time residents, the upshot is that on any night of the week
(except Mondays, when restaurateurs must all catch up on sleep or
do their laundry), we can visit one of hundreds of eateries — large
or small, pricey or cheap, fancy or not so — offering every kind
of food imaginable. Securing a reservation and the limits of your
appetite (and of your wallet) are your only constraints if you live in
this gustatory mecca.

We do go out to eat often. We love to meet family members at a
cozy area tavern for great Caesar salads topped with grilled steak or
salmon. We cherish the nights we can slip into a corner table at a
tiny local Italian restaurant, run by a talented couple who serve up
lovingly re-created dishes from the old country: pasta with shellfish,

a rich spaghetti Bolognese, or garlicky beans with sausage or kale. There is a second-story bistro in town where we can sit in a rustic wooden booth by an open window in summer, look out over the harbor, and crunch our way through an obscenely delicious platter of hot nachos smothered in guacamole, sour cream, and fresh Maine lobster. And on a blustery winter night, in one of the city's handsome, old brick factory buildings that now houses a brick-oven pizzeria, I am almost always able to score the table by the fireplace, where I toast myself back to sentience while waiting for my custom pizza heaped with spinach, mushrooms, and artichokes. And that doesn't even scratch the surface of our myriad eateries, casual to five star. For people who believe food is integrally related to happiness, health, and a sense of well-being, a town like this is a great place to live. That said, the pleasant anticipation of heading out to dinner has a flip side.

There are nights we can quickly be convinced the effort is beyond us. First, there is getting dressed in something presentable — remember, I am a writer. You don't want to know what passes for acceptable at-home fashion when I am working at my desk. There is bundling up in overcoats and heading out into what, for about half the year, can be frigidly cold temperatures, challenging parking, and dicey footing. Then there is the issue of night driving, and night driving if you want to enjoy a glass of wine or two with dinner. We also have a growing number of establishments who have joined the trend toward not accepting reservations for parties under six or eight or ten, so it's possible you will not be seated on a weekend or holiday night when you finally do arrive. Ergo, there are many nights when it doesn't take much for us to convince ourselves to hunker down at home. We cook up a simple supper, enjoy a drink by the fire while watching the evening news, and feel smugly practical and thrifty for being homebodies.

I confess that we often buy specialty foods and sometimes overpay for certain delicacies we enjoy. It's an indulgence many of us choose over new clothes, redecorating, or frequent travel and entertainment. But I also inherited my Depression-era parents' horror of wasted food. I am infamous for concocting meals from uninspiring leftovers: bits of meat or cooked vegetables, chopped and stir-fried with some cold rice; or beans and sausage simmered into a stew with a can of diced tomatoes from the pantry. There are endless things you can put into a frittata, and I never met a soup that could not assimilate some cold boiled potatoes, or the last few sautéed mushrooms from last night's steak dinner. Almost anything can be spread on slices of French bread, sprinkled with cheese, and toasted for a quick lunch or hot hors d'oeuvre. I take a perverse pleasure in these resuscitations and, so far, have not landed anyone in the emergency room.

I originally heard the essence of the following recipe on our local National Public Radio station, one evening as I was driving home from work. It was during the seemingly endless recession that pervaded nearly every aspect of life between 2005 and 2010. As I recall, the objective of the broadcast was to provide listeners with a recipe for feeding a family of four for under $10. Since I was at the wheel, I did not write down the recipe, but the idea of its parsimony pleased me. Plus it featured two of my favorite ingredients: chickpeas and spinach. I gathered the gist of it from the radio and, after numerous attempts, cobbled together my own version, which I find quick, delicious, and, yes, very inexpensive to make. I believe the NPR guest said that the dish was originally a frugal

Spanish housewife's budget-stretching family supper. I have found that it can serve as a hearty side dish to any simple grilled meat or fish, or constitute a complete meal in itself — especially

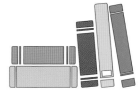

when topped with fried eggs, as described below, which is how I would serve it for book club night.

The recipe here uses canned chickpeas, which should be well rinsed in cold water and completely drained to get rid of too much salt and any canned taste. The dish is all the better if you have time to soak and cook dried garbanzo beans (use about ½ lb. dried beans for this recipe). But in the interest of time, canned chickpeas are perfectly fine. Either way, it's an earthy, filling, and healthful dish for those first cool evenings of fall, and one that won't break the bank.

• SPANISH CHICKPEAS WITH SPINACH •

2 large (13–15 oz.) cans garbanzo beans/chickpeas, rinsed in cold water and drained
Chicken broth, to cover — about 1 1/2 cups
4 tbsp. olive oil
4 large cloves garlic, minced
1/2 cup coarse bread crumbs or croutons
1 tbsp. sherry
3 tbsp. good red wine vinegar
2 tbsp. paprika
1 tsp. ground cumin
1/2 tsp. powdered thyme
1 lb. baby spinach leaves
Salt and pepper, to taste
4 or 5 large eggs (optional, 1 per person)
Fresh thyme, for garnish (if available)

Serves 6

Preparation: Place the chickpeas in a large pot, add the chicken broth — enough to just barely cover the beans — and heat through on a low burner.

While the beans are warming, heat the olive oil in a medium skillet. Add the minced garlic and brown lightly over medium heat, being careful not to burn the garlic. Turn the bread crumbs or croutons into the cooked garlic and crush with the back of a spoon to make a coarse paste. Scrape the paste from the skillet and set it aside. In the same skillet, add the sherry, vinegar, and spices and whisk all together to deglaze the pan.

Add the spinach to the chickpeas and broth, stir to submerge the spinach, and cook 2–3 minutes. Then add the garlic-bread paste and herbed vinegar mixture, and stir all gently together. Season sparingly with salt and pepper, if needed, to taste. Keep the mixture hot on a low burner.

Optional (but I think this makes the dish memorable): Heat the remaining olive oil in the skillet. Break eggs, one at a time, into a shallow dish and slide them into the hot oil. Sprinkle lightly with salt and freshly ground pepper and cook just until set.

Serve the Spanish Chickpeas with Spinach in large, shallow bowls, topping each serving with a fried egg, and garnish with a sprig of fresh thyme or other kitchen herb that may still be holding forth in your October garden. Low fat and nutritious, this is a nicely balanced and soul-satisfying dish for which I thank NPR, whether I have accurately recalled its broadcast or not. Follow the meal with good coffee, those wonderfully crisp Bosc or seasonal pears, and vanilla wafers.

NOVEMBER / THE LITERATURE OF FOOD

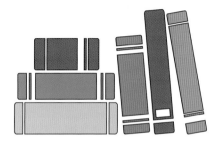

> . . . from early on, American writers have seen food as a window into the wider culture — a sign of our values and our ideals, a measure of our civilization.
>
> –Molly O'Neill, *American Food Writing*

FOR AS LONG as I can remember being able to read, I have loved reading about food. At an early age, it was clear that I loved to cook, so I read all sorts of cookbooks and recipes — from a now-antique edition of the charmingly illustrated *Kitchen Fun* by Louise Price Bell (1932) that had belonged to my mother as a child; to the surprisingly gender-neutral 1957 youth cookbook *Betty Crocker's Cook Book for Boys and Girls*, given to me by my grandmother; as well as the adult version and kitchen classic, *The Betty Crocker Cookbook*. I read these, studying the (unenhanced) photographs and illustrations, and scrutinizing the ingredients lists to see if our dull cupboard might conceivably be plundered to produce some glamorous confection.

Long before the magnificent photographic spreads in *Martha Stewart Living* magazine, I was inspired by what were, for the time, elaborately staged photographs of food — beautiful frosted layer cakes, glistening roasts, meringues piled high with strawberries and whipped cream. But I hungered equally for the scant descriptions of how, when, and why one would serve a particular dish: *for a stick-to your-ribs winter supper on a snowy night, or for a festive birthday lunch served outside on the lawn.* These notions excited my imagination. I was intrigued to think one could change the course of an insalubrious winter night by conjuring up a rich beef stew or chicken fricassee. One could script a happy birthday by making crabmeat salad and a lemon cake, then moving it all outside to be enjoyed "on the lawn." I expect I knew it would take more than crabmeat piled into an avocado to soothe my fractious family, but I somehow held out hope that if I actually reproduced these staged settings, we might be miraculously transformed. The writing was simple and the recipes often bland, but they suggested a world of pleasure, conviviality, and, somehow, control over one's environment that was appealing.

My mother did not love to cook and did so only dutifully. Our family of two parents and three girls was routinely hungry, so my culinary experiments were indulged and — despite the inevitable eye rolling from my siblings — even enjoyed when successful. As my kitchen forays became more ambitious — crêpes suzette, braided yeast breads, raised doughnuts, filled omelets, and *coq au vin* — my mother developed the notion that I should go to Cornell University's School of Hospitality (now called Hotel Administration), graduate, and get a job as one of those people who arrange all the pretty food in magazines. Almost 50 years and a dozen uninspired careers later, I'm not sure she was all that far off the mark. I might have been

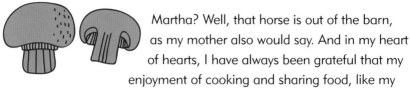

Martha? Well, that horse is out of the barn, as my mother also would say. And in my heart of hearts, I have always been grateful that my enjoyment of cooking and sharing food, like my passion for poetry and literature, remains a deeply personal pleasure and is not the profession by which I am consigned to earn my living. How much fun can it be if someone expects a perfect soufflé? About as much as if someone demanded a heartrending poem.

It was some years later, when I was out of college and living on a shoestring in New York, that I discovered there was indeed a *literature* of food — food writing beyond cookbooks and recipes. I was reading M. F. K. Fisher's work in a small compendium of her *New Yorker* pieces, titled *As They Were*. Her *truite au bleu* essay — of solitary, overheated gourmandise in a tiny, out-of-the-way restaurant in the French countryside — took my breath away. In another essay, she wrote so exquisitely of making a simple mushroom soup that I had to set the book down, grab my purse, and rush to the corner greengrocer at nine o'clock at night to buy fresh mushrooms, cream, butter, parsley, and a bottle of cold white wine to go with my impromptu soup. I raced home, delighted with my mission and with my late-night supper *à la* M. F. K.

I continue to indulge my fervor for good food writing with the works of an ever-expanding community of writers who share my enthusiasms. The homely heritage of the humdrum cookbook, the ladies magazine, and tin box of recipe cards has given way to a rich literature of food. Celebrity chefs share their secrets. Home cooks have stepped out of the shadows. Food writers today celebrate how we grow, purchase, prepare, and eat our food as a vital part of our identities. They explore food as heritage, politics, economics, love, health, and artistry, and we are all cooking and eating better for it.

november reads

Here are a few books that are rich with writings about food. I am glad to own them all. I shelve them in the kitchen, where I can turn to them for inspiration and companionship. They are spattered and stained, scribbled in, and stuffed with notes and recipes. Together with my library of cookbooks, they form a sort of archive of how I have spent a large and pleasurable amount of time in my life.

Diana Abu-Jaber, *The Language of Baklava*
A delightfully original memoir of growing up with a Jordanian immigrant father, obsessed with the foods of his native Bedouin culture, and an American mother. Abu-Jaber writes sensuously and lovingly of the baklava, shish kebabs, Arabic dishes, and ubiquitous spices and scents of her culinary heritage. A story of family, love, and the food that feeds our souls.

Erica Bauermeister, *The School of Essential Ingredients*
Bauermeister's best-selling first novel. It is the story of Lillian, who holds a monthly cooking class for eight very different students at her Pacific Northwest restaurant. With each of the classes and the foods the amateur cooks learn to prepare and savor, character studies of the students and their teacher emerge, as they heal and satisfy themselves through shared time in the kitchen.

Frank Bruni, *Born Round: A Story of Family, Food, and a Ferocious Appetite*
Former *New York Times* restaurant critic Bruni's engaging story of his journey from growing up a chubby, always-hungry little boy to becoming one of the most influential figures in the restaurant world. Bruni's love-hate relationship with food and his battle of the bulge will ring true to anyone who's ever wrestled with an eating disorder or an overly healthy appetite.

Bill Buford, *Heat: An Amateur's Adventures as a Kitchen Slave*
   The acclaimed author and *New Yorker* fiction editor takes time
   off to realize a long-held dream of becoming a professional
   chef, by apprenticing himself out to such restaurant luminaries
   as Mario Batali. Along the way, he lands in some of the most
   celebrated kitchens in the world, taking us behind the scenes
   with his signature wit, self-deprecating humor, and, finally, some
   real kitchen wisdom.

Julia Child with Alex Prud'homme, *My Life in France*
   Julia's own story of arriving in France, a complete novice in the
   kitchen and unable to speak passable French. Her decision to
   enroll in classes at the famed Le Cordon Bleu, and her ensuing
   passion for French cookery, changed the course of culinary
   history in America.

Laurie Colwin, *Home Cooking* and *More Home Cooking*
   The late novelist and food writer's two winning and
   unpretentious chronicles of teaching herself to cook and
   entertain — from epic dinner-party failures to richly satisfying
   family meals and holiday parties for her young daughter and
   friends. As much memoirs as cookbooks, Colwin's now-classic
   duo are witty and lovable kitchen companions for anyone who
   wants to cook and loves to read.

M. F. K. Fisher, *The Gastronomical Me, How to Cook a Wolf, As
They Were, A Cordiall Water,* and others
   Any work by the preeminent American food and travel writer
   inspires both the literary and the culinary imagination. Fisher
   believed that eating well was one of the "arts of life," and she
    wrote 27 remarkable books, as well as countless
   articles and essays, celebrating a life rich with food,
   travel, and culture. Her sharp, sensitive prose is
   among the most admired in the English language,

and almost anything she sets to paper still stands as the *ne plus ultra* of a literature that celebrates good food as an essential element of a good life.

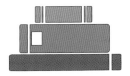

Daniel Halpern, *Not for Bread Alone: Writers on Food, Wine, and the Art of Eating*

A compilation of food writing by 22 noted authors, from Charles Lamb to Alice Waters, edited by the distinguished poet Daniel Halpern. Widely divergent in style and subject, these essays collectively explore the ritual, romance, and human implications of what and how we feed ourselves and those around us.

Gabrielle Hamilton, *Blood, Bones & Butter: The Inadvertent Education of a Reluctant Chef*

An eye-opening memoir of trial, error, and eventual success by the owner/chef of New York's celebrated Prune Restaurant. From her Pennsylvania childhood — growing up with a French mother who was always at the stove with a dripping spoon in her hand, and a mercurial artist father who congregated his community for bacchanalian feasts — to her youthful travels in Europe as a half-starved teenager and her audacious move to open her own New York City restaurant, Hamilton's saga is relentlessly honest, wry, gritty, and full of passion for her subject and her profession.

Madhur Jaffrey, *Climbing the Mango Trees: A Memoir of a Childhood in India*

A mesmerizing memoir by an actress, author, and culinary authority on Indian cuisine and tradition. Born in 1933, Jaffrey grew up the daughter of a prosperous Hindu family in Delhi, where family meals were often sumptuous affairs served to 40 or more family members. In her memoir, Jaffrey evokes the rich spices and fragrant foods of her childhood and a way of life that would be lost after the political upheaval and strife of partition.

Judith Jones, *The Tenth Muse: My Life in Food*

An enlightening behind-the-scenes memoir from the legendary editor of Julia Child's *Mastering the Art of French Cooking*. Jones writes with warmth and affection of her relationships with such culinary luminaries as James Beard, Lidia Bastianich, Madhur Jaffrey, and the great M. F. K. Fisher — revering them as authors, friends, and inspirations.

Nicole Mones, *The Last Chinese Chef*

Maggie, a widowed American food writer, travels to Beijing to investigate a Chinese paternity claim against her late husband's estate, and to profile a rising star Chinese chef, Sam Liang, for her magazine. As she follows Sam and his relatives through the rigors of the Chinese National Cooking Olympics, Maggie is drawn into the mystique, poetry, passion, and *guanxi*, or "connectedness," that binds Chinese history to its foods. Rich with mouth-watering descriptions of exquisitely prepared dishes.

Molly O'Neill, *One Big Table*

The *New York Times* food columnist's trans-American road trip to research the alleged decline of home cooking in America. The substantial book that resulted is a celebration of hometown specialties, intergenerational family dishes, and the glorious and curious culinary diversities of America at the table.

Julia Reed, *Ham Biscuits, Hostess Gowns, and Other Southern Specialties: An Entertaining Life (with Recipes)*

A witty and engaging essay collection on the very particular customs, quirks, and charms of Southern cooking, entertaining, and famous Southern hospitality. Whether elucidating such Southern classics as crabmeat canapés and red velvet cake, or offering up her own variations on regional favorites, Reed writes with warmth, humor, and a certain Southern charm.

Ruth Reichl, *Tender at the Bone, Comfort Me with Apples*, and *Garlic and Sapphires*

> A kind of trilogy of love, life, and memorable meals, by the celebrated *New York Times* restaurant critic and memoirist. In stories both hilarious and reverent — from growing up in the age of the organic food revolution to adventures in dining with world-famous chefs and her life as an undercover restaurant critic, costumed and disguised for anonymity — Reichl brilliantly chronicles the evolution, genius, and foibles of America's gustatory coming of age.

Calvin Trillin, *Alice, Let's Eat*

> America's funniest food writer embarks on a hilarious odyssey for "something decent to eat." From his colorful and often unlikely dining companions to his hole-in-the-wall culinary discoveries, Trillin is insatiably driven in his mission and never less than inspired as a humorist.

Various Editors, *Best Food Writing* annual anthologies

> Published annually since 2000, 14 anthologies of each year's best food writing. Featuring celebrity chefs, established food writers, cutting-edge bloggers, and up-and-coming new voices, the collections are always a worthwhile sampling of evolving American tastes, trends, and eating adventures for foodies.

on the menu

ITALIAN MINESTRONE SOUP

*Good soups I hold in as high regard as great breads,
and together they make some of life's sublime moments*

–Anna Thomas, *The Vegetarian Epicure*

I would be hard-pressed to name my favorite soup. I am crazy for almost any steaming bowl of broth filled with vegetables, bits of meat, beans, pasta, or potatoes. I love smooth cream soups, redolent with the essential flavors of mushrooms, celery, or cool cucumber in summer. And there are few things more satisfying than a soup based on legumes: rich white bean and bacon, Cuban black bean laced with sherry, split pea and ham, or a sturdy lentil soup. I would not want to be told I could never again savor the pleasure of a New England clam, corn, or fresh fish chowder. When I have a cold or sore throat, there is nothing better than chicken soup with a generous squeeze of fresh lemon juice — a quick-fix kind of Greek *avgolemono* or egg-lemon soup. When you've been off your feed with a stomach bug, clear beef bouillon is the first step back to the world of the living.

Good soups are all soothing and fortifying in their own way, and they require little in the way of equipment besides a deep stockpot and a good chopping knife and board. (I would also put in a word for an immersion or hand blender, a wonderful gadget I have come to rely on for smooth or partially blended soups, but you can also purée ingredients in a blender or food processor in batches. An immersion blender just makes it a cinch.)

If I had to choose just one recipe that embodies the multiple fine qualities of all soups, it would probably be the classic Italian minestrone. And it must be made from scratch. I am not a purist when it comes to necessary shortcuts involving a can of Campbell's cream of mushroom or celery soup to enrich a chicken stew or help out your stroganoff, but here you cannot let yourself be satisfied with the watery and oversalted canned minestrones on the market. The real deal is a festival of color, textures, and flavors that can only be achieved with authentic ingredients and a little effort. Truth be told, I think I like making soups as much as eating them. On a chilly November afternoon, I love chopping up all the different vegetables for minestrone and dumping them into a big stockpot with herbs, beans, and pasta to simmer and fill the house with the aroma of something delicious in the making. I like settling down with a good book, anticipating a meal of this soul-satisfying Mediterranean feast with some crusty bread and a glass of red wine. It makes a perfect cool-weather meal for your book group, and you will enjoy any leftovers as much or more than the first serving.

There are many variables for the perfect minestrone, but this recipe covers all the basics — vegetables, beans, small pasta, and a rich tomato base — as well as a few of those elements, such as shredded greens, that I find very satisfying in this healthful meal in a bowl. Like many hearty soups, it is arguably better made a day in advance and chilled overnight to let its various flavors meld. I have also become convinced that the Continental practice of tossing an aged Parmesan cheese rind into the pot is a wonderful refinement. You pay dearly for your wedge of good Parmigiano-Reggiano at the market, so why not use every last crumb? It gives the soup a deep, rich flavor — just remember to fish out the softened rind before serving.

• ITALIAN MINESTRONE SOUP •

2 tbsp. olive oil
1 large onion, chopped
2 cloves garlic, peeled and minced
4 stalks celery, chopped into ½" pieces
4 large carrots, chopped into ½" pieces
6–7 cups chicken, beef*, or vegetable stock (or a combination)
1 large (27 oz.) can diced tomatoes
Rind of Parmigiano-Reggiano, for the pot
⅔ cup small pasta, such as elbows or seashells
2 medium zucchini, sliced into rounds and cut into quarter rounds
2 medium summer squash, sliced into rounds and cut into quarter rounds
2 cups (about 25) fresh green beans, trimmed and cut into 1" pieces
1 good-sized bunch fresh kale, chard, collards, mustard greens, or
    other coarse greens (or a mixture of several), stems and tough leaves
    removed, shredded into ribbons about 1"–2" long
1 can chickpeas
1 can red kidney beans
½ cup chopped fresh basil
2 tsp. dried oregano
2 tbsp. good red wine vinegar
Freshly grated Parmesan, for serving

*I like to use half beef stock and half vegetable stock for this soup base,
    but if you are serving to strict vegetarians, vegetable stock is fine.

Serves 6

Preparation: Heat oil in a large stockpot. Add chopped onion
and minced garlic and cook until onions are translucent, about
5–7 minutes, stirring often. Add chopped celery and carrots and
cook until slightly softened, about 5 minutes. Add broth and diced

tomatoes and bring to a simmer. Add Parmigiano-Reggiano rind. Simmer together for 15 minutes.

Add pasta to boiling broth and cook until barely al dente, about 4 minutes, stirring often to keep pasta from sticking together.

Add in zucchini, summer squash, green beans, and shredded greens. Return to boil and continue to simmer on low for 10–15 minutes. Fold in chickpeas, kidney beans, basi, and oregano. Add vinegar and heat through. Check seasoning and add a small amount of broth or water if soup is too thick. Simmer all together for 5–7 minutes.

Ideally, this soup should be made a day ahead and refrigerated overnight to bring out its full flavor. Cool completely to room temperature, then cover tightly and chill overnight. Reheat gently on low, checking the liquid level and stirring often so the bottom of the pot does not scald. Add a small amount of water if the broth needs thinning.

Before serving, fish out the cheese rind with a slotted spoon. Ladle the minestrone into large soup platters and top with freshly grated Parmesan cheese.

Minestrone is a complete meal in itself and needs only a good crusty bread and glass of wine to perfect the experience. Espresso, served with a twist of lemon, and cannoli or another filled pastry from your local Italian bakery would make a perfectly authentic finish to a supper of minestrone.

DECEMBER / THE LIVES OF OTHERS

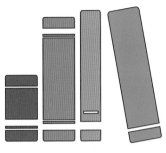

We should look for someone to eat and drink with
before looking for something to eat and drink . . .

–Epicurus

WHEN DECEMBER ROLLS around in our southern Maine city, I can
sense the heightening level of activity and excitement in my local
bookstore. Aisles are blocked by dolly carts stacked with boxes of new
books. Unfamiliar holiday help appears behind the cash registers,
window displays are freshened up, and the checkout counter is
dense with "impulse purchase" displays of novelty books, pocket
calendars, sparkly pens, and luxurious, cloth-covered diaries. The
handsome new hardback best-sellers are stacked ten deep on the
shelves, and dozens of enticing titles are featured as "Staff Picks." I
love to read the employees' handwritten recommendations scrawled
on bookmarks. I know a lot of the staff at my bookstore, so their
opinions mean something to me. There are always some big-name or
critically acclaimed books being released just in time for the holidays.
If I have read one or more of them, I feel somehow reassured that I

am making a stab at keeping current with literature, new ideas, and the lightning pace of change in the world. Most of us will buy and give multiple gifts this month. Your local bookseller wants that gift to be a book.

When I receive the gift of a book, I know that someone cared enough to spend time in a bookstore (or online, yes, but time is time), trying to think of what I would like to read. They have had to wonder if I've read it already, if it will appeal to me. They will read the dust jacket, the first pages, and ask the store owner for recommendations. I know, because I go through all these steps when I buy books for friends and family. To give a book implies that you respect the recipient as someone who can appreciate the shared journey of another's story.

Among my own favorite gifted books was one I received from a former roommate many years ago. I was studying (and I use the term loosely) abroad, taking a class in poetry and poetry writing. Just before the holidays, she sent me the small, blue-paper-covered, letterpress edition of Dylan Thomas's exquisite prose poem, *A Child's Christmas in Wales*, illustrated with simple woodcuts. Our class had been assigned to write a poem in the style of a poet we had studied, so I wrote and read aloud a Christmas prose poem of my own making, "in the style of" Thomas. It was clunky and sentimental, but I had put my heart into it. Reading it aloud to my classmates eased our vague collective homesickness. Writing it made me want to be a poet.

Most book groups embrace their December gathering as a time to celebrate. One group I know asks members to bring or talk about a favorite book they received as a gift, or discuss the book(s) they would most like to receive. Some great gift ideas have been shared in this manner, as well as possible prospects for the next year's book group selections.

december reads

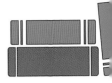

The holiday season, for all its commercial distortions, remains the time of year to think of others, whether through charity, visits, gifts, or simple kindnesses. When it comes to our reading choices, it can be an ideal time to immerse ourselves in the lives of others — biographies, autobiographies, memoirs, accounts of historical events written by those who lived them firsthand. Whenever we take the time to learn another's life story, we emerge a bit more empathic for having stepped outside ourselves to follow the road traveled by a fellow human being. Here is a list of some outstanding life stories to read, to give as gifts, and/or to share with your book group. All are memorable human histories with the power to inspire and transform.

Stephen Ambrose, *Undaunted Courage: Meriwether Lewis, Thomas Jefferson, and the Opening of the American West*
> Ambrose's definitive history of Lewis and Clark's 1803 expedition to map the unknown territories eventually claimed for the continental United States under the Louisiana Purchase. Rich with scholarly detail, drama, and suspense, as well as a remarkable cast of political and military figures, naturalists, hunters and traders, Indian chiefs, and the girl guide Sacagawea, this is an enthralling account of America's most significant land exploration.

Maya Angelou, *I Know Why the Caged Bird Sings*
> Angelou's debut memoir of growing up in a small Southern town in an era rife with bigotry and darkened by familial abandonment. A stunning work of personal courage, poetry, and self-discovery, readers took Angelou into their hearts with this book and secured its position in the canon of American letters.

Robert Caro, *The Power Broker: Robert Moses and the Fall of New York*
The Pulitzer Prize–winning exposé of Moses's behind-the-scenes maneuverings to shape modern-day New York City, and the unstoppable political machine he controlled. Nelson Rockefeller emerges as the only man of equal will and power who could stand up to Moses.

Joan Didion, *The Year of Magical Thinking*
A memoir of one year in the life of iconic American essayist Joan Didion, following the sudden death of her husband of 40 years, writer John Gregory Dunne, while their only daughter lies gravely ill in the hospital. Written with characteristic candor, eloquence, and humanity, Didion's clear-eyed account is a moving tribute to her life with the late Dunne, and to the necessity of moving beyond grief.

Doris Kearns Goodwin, *Lyndon Johnson and the American Dream*
As a former member of Johnson's White House staff, Goodwin delivers an incisive biography of the larger-than-life president. Sworn in to the office of president immediately following the incomprehensible assassination of JFK in 1963, Johnson governed a traumatized country through the turbulent '60s, the Vietnam War, and, notably, passage of the Voting Rights Act, wielding his own brand of power and influence in pursuit of his objectives.

Katharine Graham, *Personal History*
The autobiography of Katharine "Kay" Graham, heiress to a family fortune and inheritor of the once-struggling *Washington Post*. Kay and her husband, the brilliant and troubled Phil Graham, and eventually their son, assume the reins of the D.C. paper, most famously working with Ben Bradlee through the Watergate scandal and decades of American political history.

Alex Haley and Malcolm X, *The Autobiography of Malcolm X: As Told to Alex Haley*

> The searing autobiography of the converted Muslim leader, agitator, and civil rights maverick who formed the Organization of Afro-American Unity in the 1960s, inspiring Americans to pursue black pride, power, and equality. A powerful portrait of a man whose movement is still being lived out on America's streets today.

Walter Isaacson, *Steve Jobs*

> Written with the cooperation of his subject and published posthumously, the story of Steve Jobs's genius and relentless drive for perfection in the connection of art to technology. A counterculture rebel who became a billionaire, his story is revealed in hours of personal interviews and conversations with those who knew and worked with him.

David McCullough, *Mornings on Horseback*

> Master historian and storyteller David McCullough's fascinating biography of Teddy Roosevelt, a sickly child with chronic asthma who transformed himself into a vigorous outdoorsman, fearless war hero, and, ultimately, president of the United States. McCullough breathes immediacy, drama, and humanity into his larger-than-life subject.

Siddhartha Mukherjee, *The Emperor of All Maladies: A Biography of Cancer*

> An extraordinary work of medical and scientific research and scholarship, tracing the history of a disease humans have lived with and combatted for over 5,000 years. A surprisingly readable narrative about this most intensely studied but still misunderstood disease. Winner of the Pulitzer Prize.

Barack Obama, *The Audacity of Hope*

President Obama's 2006 "Thoughts on
Reclaiming the American Dream." Calling
for a new brand of politics and a fresh
approach to issues of race, community, and American identity,
Obama writes movingly of his own family story and the values
that shaped his extraordinary journey to the U.S. Senate and his
eventual and successful bid for the White House.

Stacy Schiff, *Cleopatra: A Life*
A new look at the infamous Egyptian queen. Distorted by
historians as a manipulative femme fatale, Schiff's compelling
narrative delivers an entirely new portrait of a woman who's not
afraid to exploit her talents nor her appetite for sexual intrigue.

Rebecca Skloot, *The Immortal Life of Henrietta Lacks*
The story of a poor black tobacco farmer whose untimely cancer
cells were taken without her knowledge in 1951. Known only to the
scientific community as HeLa cells, they became the Holy Grail of
medical research and vital to the development of the polio vaccine,
cloning, genetic research, and more. Virtually unknown until this
best-seller, Henrietta's story is an unprecedented look at medical
ethics, race, poverty, and the generational bonds of family.

Emily Spivack, *Worn Stories*
Artist and editor, Emily Spivack's collection of over 60 clothing-
inspired personal narratives, written by well-known cultural
figures (Susan Orlean, Rosanne Cash, designer Cynthia Rowley,
Piper Kerman, Greta Gerwig, Heidi Julavits, and others) as well
as everyday storytellers. *Worn Stories* unfurls a wide-ranging and
fascinating look at how clothing expresses, protects, and masks
identities, ultimately becoming mementos imbued with our
unique life histories.

Gertrude Stein, *The Autobiography of Alice B. Toklas*
In 1932, largely to amuse herself, the poet and writer Stein wrote this irreverent, conversational biography of her companion of 25 years, Alice B. Toklas. Unlike any biography written before, it affords a unique window on the literary and artistic Golden Age of Paris between the wars, and on two of its most influential personalities.

Cheryl Strayed, *Wild: From Lost to Found on the Pacific Crest Trail*
In the wake of her mother's death, author Strayed finds her life unraveling. After a divorce and four years of self-destructive behavior, Strayed makes the impulsive decision to hike more than 1,000 miles of the Pacific Crest Trail — alone, in an effort to contemplate her grief and what has become of her life. Written with wit, verve, and unflinching honesty, Strayed's harrowing odyssey to personal redemption is a powerful statement of human determination and courage.

Elie Wiesel, *Night*
One of the most important books of the 20th century and perhaps the definitive work of Holocaust literature. Wiesel's masterpiece is a candid and impassioned account of his daily survival in the death camps of Auschwitz and Buchenwald. Beyond bearing witness to the sadistic horrors inflicted by his Nazi captors, Wiesel probes the deepest psychological questions of how inhumanity could be perpetrated on such a monstrous scale, and what the Holocaust's legacy for future generations will be.

on the menu

HOLIDAY BELLS

If more of us valued food and cheer and song
above hoarded gold, it would be a merrier world.

–J. R. R. Tolkien, author of *The Lord of the Rings trilogy*

December before the solstice: long, hushed nights, sometimes
muffled by snow — nights that don't seem to end, if you have to
rise in the dark. Who doesn't burrow down deeper at the alarm
clock's insistent predawn decree? When I had to appear at my
desk in town at an early hour, I thought those dim winter mornings
particularly unkind. After the solstice, there is hope: mornings and
evenings will become lighter, but the light is miserly in coming.
It would be good to be a bear.

I no longer keep that schedule, but find I still rise early. I have also
come to a kind of truce with chilly winter mornings, and most days, I
actually enjoy them. I like slipping downstairs in the half-dark, trailed
by our cats, Lily and Violet. I like the hush of the house, the clanking
of the heat coming up, and the burbling of the coffeemaker. I like
looking out over the frozen yard to the orange streaks of the sunrise
on the horizon. Usually I'll check the thermometer on the kitchen
window and the direction of the wind sock flapping on its pole affixed
to the back fence. Sometimes a perfect new cover of snow has fallen
overnight or may still be falling. I'll flip on the light by the back door
so the cats and I can take stock of the accumulation and what will
need to be shoveled later on. They are indoor cats and sisters, but
both take a healthy interest in the tenacious chickadees, cardinals,

and jays that frequent the winter bird feeder. Cats wake up slowly, yawning, stretching, grooming themselves and each other. Early mornings are my slow waking-up time too, my quiet hour or so to order my thoughts for the day.

The first and most momentous task of any day is to feed Lily and Violet before they wander off to some invisible distraction. We make quite a fuss of it, opening cans and tapping spoons on the dish. If I've promoted their breakfast properly, they'll eat for a bit, then vanish for hours. I can then turn to human affairs. Every morning, I drink a tall glass of water with half a lemon squeezed in it. I've done this forever on the theory that it's healthier for me than sugary fruit juice. Also because my paternal grandmother, who lived to be a healthy 97, always started her day this way. Of course, she did a lot of other things too — like never having an alcoholic drink in her life. Stay tuned.

I try to keep a good supply of fresh fruit on hand that I'll slice up in a big glass bowl for our breakfasts. If possible, I try to buy produce that is grown in the United States, not flown in from Chile or South Africa. In December, that means some combination of Florida grapefruit, oranges, tangerines, blood oranges (which add great drama), or little rings of kumquat that I adore. Sometimes I'll add a pear or a banana for counterpoint. A college friend recently introduced me to Asian pears, which grew in abundance on her tree in Massachusetts. I have become a convert — crisp, juicy, and smooth textured, they are a wonderful discovery. All of the citrus peelings and my squeezed lemon then get dumped into a saucepan and covered with hot water. I add a good jolt of cloves, cinnamon, nutmeg, or something like allspice or pumpkin pie spice — whatever I can put my hand on in the spice rack that looks warm and fragrant.

I set this hodgepodge to boil on the stove while I finish setting out our breakfast. Known in our family as "stovetop boil," it's a great DIY to freshen the air in a house closed up for winter and makes a welcoming kitchen for your family in the morning. The boiling fruit skins and spices give off a clean, aromatic steam that is reminiscent of the pomander balls we used to make for Christmas — apples, oranges, or lemons stuck with hundreds of whole cloves, then wrapped in cheesecloth with cinnamon and orris root to dry, before being tied up with ribbons to hang. (The boiling method is an infinitely easier route to manufacture this perfume.) With the kitchen warm and spicy, the cats fed, the coffee hot, and breakfast on the table, winter mornings start to look more bearable.

Whether it's sticking cloves into oranges, decorating cookies with kids, or caroling around the neighborhood, we all have our own holiday traditions, large and small, and want to share them with others when we celebrate special occasions. So many little rituals of the seasons are tied to our own selective memories and idiosyncrasies, it's hard to know what gestures and customs truly connect with others. The season is rife with stories of elaborately planned events or family celebrations run amok with children in tears and exhausted adults headed for bed or the bar. It's probably wise not to get too ambitious with plans for a five-course dinner for 50 at this busy time of year. But some festive activity or a modest gathering is part of how we celebrate the winter solstice, the passing of another year, and our various December holidays. So if you don't jump in with both feet, at least put a toe in the water. Go ice skating on the pond and warm up with some hot chocolate. Drop in on a neighbor with a holiday plant, or nab your spouse for a neighborhood tour of light displays, then drop by the local tavern for a drink by the fire. It doesn't have to be much, but it has to be *something*. And some part of your gesture is bound to rub off on even the most circumspect members of your household or bah-humbug friends. It's like adult birthdays: doing nothing can itself give you the blues.

For some monthly book groups, the December gathering includes spouses and partners. It's a way to thank them for supporting the time we spend with our group and their understanding when we each host a gathering. It's also just a good excuse for us all to be together for a relaxed evening. Sometimes my group has been fancy and held a multicourse dinner seated at the table. Some years we just have a small cocktail party with lots of finger foods. One year we shared an elegant homemade Chanukah dinner of beet soup, potato pancakes with applesauce, challah bread, and flourless chocolate cake, followed by a marathon session of what was dubbed a "dreidel slam."

Here is a simple dish that makes a festive group meal for the holidays — or almost any time. I have made it in warm months and served it at room temperature with a side of chilled cucumbers and sour cream, and it was delicious. In cold weather, serve it piping hot with a side salad of greens and orange slices lightly dressed and sprinkled with toasted almonds. You can assemble this dish up to a day ahead, wrap it tightly, and refrigerate. Pop it in a preheated oven about an hour before you plan to seat guests at the table. I use red and green peppers here for their holiday colors. You could substitute a combination of red, yellow, and orange peppers for summer or fall platters.

• HOLIDAY BELLS •

2 large red bell peppers
2 large green bell peppers
1 ½ cups white rice
3 tbsp. olive oil, plus more for drizzling
2 large cloves garlic, minced
1 medium onion, chopped fine
1 15 oz. can diced tomatoes
1 10 oz. pkg. frozen chopped spinach, thawed and water pressed out
1 small jar chopped pimientos
1 tsp. oregano
1 cup frozen petite peas, thawed
2 cups loosely packed fresh crabmeat*
Salt and freshly ground pepper
½ cup fine bread crumbs
½ cup grated Parmesan cheese
¼ cup chopped fresh leaf parsley
Fresh herbs, for garnish (rosemary or sage for holiday platters; fresh basil on summer plates)

*If you cannot find or do not like crabmeat, you can use 1 lb. small salad shrimp, shelled, rinsed, and tails removed.

Serves 6–8

Preparation: Preheat oven to 350°F (175°C).

Wash peppers and cut them in half from stem to base, removing the inner pulp and seeds. Rinse and place, skin side down, in a large baking dish or lasagna pan that can go straight to the table.

Prepare rice according to directions, adding 1 tablespoon olive oil to the water. Remove from heat, toss with a fork, and set aside.

While rice is cooking, heat remaining 2 tablespoons olive oil in a deep skillet. Add garlic and onion and cook until onion is translucent, about 5 minutes. Add tomatoes, chopped spinach, pimientos, and oregano. Combine gently and bring just to a simmer for 8–10 minutes. Fold in peas and rice, and heat through. Gently fold in crabmeat. Add salt and pepper as needed. If the mixture has too much liquid, cook uncovered briefly to boil it off; if it's too dry, add a small amount of broth or water. The mixture should be moist but hold its shape.

Fill each half-pepper shell with the rice mixture, mounding the mixture on top with a spoon. Sprinkle each pepper lightly with bread crumbs, grated cheese, and fresh parsley. Bake for 30–40 minutes, until the cheese is golden and peppers are soft and lightly browned. Allow to set for 5–7 minutes before serving. If you are serving on another platter, lift peppers gently with a spatula onto your serving platter (white shows off the colors best for a holiday table) and garnish the platter with fresh herbs.

If you wish, serve with a side salad of thinly sliced cucumber (use the slice side of your grater) tossed with a blend of mayonnaise, sour cream, and dill. Add a basket of lightly toasted bread rounds, and you are set to go.

postscript

I am going to give you one last menu of two parts, simply because these dishes comprise one of my all-time favorite meals to serve, and I could not decide where to place them in this book. I have found the combination to be delicious any time of year and infinitely flexible, and everybody is delighted with it when they sit down to the table. I have served it on cold winter nights to family arriving after a long car trip. And I have served it on muddy March evenings when its hints of the tropics are lively and cheering.

The dishes are Caribbean Corn Chowder and Shrimp Quesadillas. To me, they go together perfectly. The chowder is a light, tomato-based soup with summery ingredients. The quesadillas add substance and crunch to the meal and should be served with the traditional sides of sour cream and salsa. In cold weather, they make for a bright-colored, warm-flavored meal that can be made ahead and casually served. In warm weather, the soup can be served cold and the quesadillas at room temperature. If you can get fresh corn and dill in summer months, so much the better, but the recipes will not suffer from pantry-shelf ingredients. Here is my current all-purpose menu for a small group, to serve any time of year:

a menu for all seasons

CARIBBEAN CORN CHOWDER

4 tbsp. olive oil
1 large sweet onion, diced
1 large red sweet pepper, diced
1 large yellow sweet pepper, diced
2 cups peeled and chopped carrots
2 cups trimmed and diced celery
4 cups chicken broth
1 24 oz. can diced tomatoes
1 tsp. dried oregano
4–5 cups sweet corn (cut from the cob, canned, or frozen)
¼ cup fresh, chopped dill, plus sprigs
Salt and pepper, to taste

Serves 6–8

Preparation: Heat olive oil in a large stockpot and add diced onions, peppers, carrots, and celery. Sauté until all are slightly softened, about 12–15 minutes. Add chicken broth, diced tomatoes, and oregano and bring to a boil. Simmer together for 10 minutes. Ladle about half the soup into a large container and set aside. Using an immersion blender*, carefully purée the remaining half of the soup in the stockpot until slightly smooth but chunky — do not overblend. Add back the rest of the soup to the stockpot, stir in the corn and fresh dill, and heat through. Season with salt and pepper to taste. May be made ahead and stored overnight to maximize flavor. Serve hot or cold, garnished with dill sprigs.

*If you don't have an immersion or hand blender, purée half the soup lightly in a food processor in batches, just pulsing it a few times before returning it to the pot.

SHRIMP QUESADILLAS

4 large white flour tortillas
Canola oil spray
1 green bell pepper, finely chopped
1 medium onion, diced
Salt and pepper
2 cups finely shredded jack cheese or Mexican blend of cheeses
1 lb. small salad shrimp, cooked and rinsed

Salsa and sour cream, to be served on the side

Serves 6–8

Preparation: (This preparation presumes you do not have a stovetop grill, which is the best place to make quesadillas. For the oven method, use cookie sheets to compress the filled tortillas. This works well and also allows you to make the quesadillas ahead and store them, stacked on the cookie sheets and separated by parchment paper, until you are ready to serve them.)

Preheat oven to 400°F (200°C).

Cover two large cookie sheets with parchment paper. Spray one side of each tortilla with canola oil (or use a brush to lightly coat) and place tortillas, oil side down, on the parchment paper. Place two tortillas on each sheet. Set aside.

Heat 2 tablespoons canola oil in a large skillet and add bell pepper and onion. Sauté until onions are translucent and peppers are soft. Season lightly with salt and pepper.

Sprinkle half of each tortilla with shredded cheese, avoiding the edges. Spoon sautéed onion and bell pepper on top of the cheese.

Sprinkle cooked shrimp over the vegetables and cover with more cheese; keep filling on just one half of each tortilla, leaving the other half plain. Fold the plain half of each tortilla over the filling and press lightly to compact. Arrange two folded tortillas evenly on each cookie sheet.

Bake tortillas 12–15 minutes, until golden brown. Remove from the oven and compress one cookie sheet of quesadillas with the second sheet for about 2 minutes, then reverse and press the other two quesadillas. To serve, cut each quesadilla into 4 wedges with a sharp chopping knife. Serve immediately, or cool and refrigerate in a stack on the cookie sheets until ready to serve.

Reheat in a 300°F (150°C) oven.

Arrange quesadilla wedges on a platter and serve with a side of salsa and sour cream.

postscript: NEW BOOKS

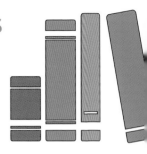

It is impossible to keep updating my favorites
lists and still turn in a final manuscript to my
publisher. And as a practical matter, I don't
need to — you and your book group will do
this each time you gather to discuss good
books and select your next read. The lists I
offer here are meant to prompt those discussions and bring your
attention to some classics you might never have found time to read,
or some titles you may not yet have discovered. I urge you to be
interactive with *Well Read, Well Fed*; add your own favorite titles to
any category, scribble notes and comments in the margins, and
make your own lists.

And I hope you will do the same for the recipes, tweaking them
and making them your own with personal additions, substitutions,
and innovations. It is no secret that you can look up and download
any one of a zillion recipes on the Internet anytime you wish.
Everyone does it sometimes, and I do too. But that is a totally
different enterprise than turning to a recipe you love and have
made a dozen times. You know exactly how much lemon juice
will wake up the flavor, that Cheddar is better than the mozzarella
cheese called for, or that using half broth and half wine makes
the sauce memorable. I would be especially pleased to think that
someday your copy of this book about reading good books and
cooking for friends is as dog-eared, stained, and personalized as

the old cookbooks, ledgers, and recipe collections I have used and reused for years. They are my record of little discoveries from a lifetime of trial-and-error cooking. They are my steadfast reading and cooking companions, and no tablet or computer can take their place.

book list: BY AUTHOR

JANUARY: WARM READS

Joe Bolton, *The Last Nostalgia: Poems 1982–1990*

Gerald Durrell, *My Family and Other Animals*

Dave Eggers, *A Hologram for the King*

John Fowles, *The Magus*

Carl Hiaasen, *Double Whammy*

Shara McCallum, *This Strange Land*

Carson McCullers, *The Member of the Wedding*

Toni Morrison, *Song of Solomon*

Pablo Neruda, *Isla Negra: A Notebook*

Ann Patchett, *State of Wonder*

Arundhati Roy, *The God of Small Things*

Karen Russell, *Swamplandia!*

Wallace Stegner, *Angle of Repose*

Derek Walcott, *Selected Poems*

FEBRUARY: LOVE STORIES

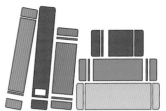

John Bayley, *Elegy for Iris*

Wendell Berry, *Hannah Coulter*

Eli Brown, *Cinnamon and Gunpowder*

Michael Cunningham, *The Hours*

Nicholas Evans, *The Horse Whisperer*

Jack Finney, *Time and Again*

John Keats, *Letters of John Keats*

Jerome Kilty, *Dear Liar*

Nicole Krauss, *The History of Love*

Ian McEwan, *Atonement*

Margaret Mitchell, *Gone with the Wind*

Michael Ondaatje, *The English Patient*

Leo Tolstoy, *Anna Karenina*

William Butler Yeats, *The Collected Poems*

MARCH: WANDERLUST

Bill Bryson, *A Walk in the Woods*

Louis De Bernieres, *Corelli's Mandolin*

M. F. K. Fisher, *The Boss Dog*

Lily King, *Euphoria*

Rosemary Mahoney, *Down the Nile*

Czeslaw Milosz, *New and Collected Poems*

Michael Paterniti, *The Telling Room*

Audrey Schulman, *Three Weeks in December*

Mary Ann Shaffer and Annie Barrows, *The Guernsey Literary and Potato Peel Pie Society*

Janet Wallach, *Desert Queen*

APRIL: FUNNY PAGES

Alan Bennett, *The Uncommon Reader*

Bill Bryson, *The Life and Times of the Thunderbolt Kid*

Helen Fielding, *Bridget Jones's Diary*

Carl Hiaasen, *Tourist Season*

David Sedaris, *Me Talk Pretty One Day*

Maria Semple, *Where'd You Go, Bernadette*

Kevin Wilson, *The Family Fang*

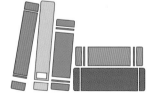

MAY: ESSAYS AND MEMOIR

Russell Baker, *Growing Up*

Roz Chast, *Can't We Talk About Something More Pleasant?*

Jill Ker Conway, *The Road from Coorain*

Joan Didion, *The White Album*

M. F. K. Fisher, *As They Were*

Mary Karr, *The Liars' Club*

Maxine Kumin, *Women, Animals, and Vegetables*

Kim Dana Kupperman, *I Just Lately Started Buying Wings*

Anna Quindlen, *Thinking Out Loud*

Penelope Schwartz Robinson, *Slippery Men*

Dustin Beall Smith, *Key Grip*

Monica Wood, *When We Were the Kennedys*

Baron Wormser, *The Road Washes Out in Spring*

JUNE: LITERARY FICTION

James Agee, *A Death in the Family*

Margaret Atwood, *The Handmaid's Tale*

Elizabeth Bishop, *The Poems of Elizabeth Bishop*

Tracy Chevalier, *Girl with a Pearl Earring*

Andre Dubus III, *House of Sand and Fog*

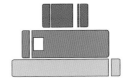

Louise Erdrich, *The Round House*

Jeffrey Eugenides, *Middlesex*

Sue Monk Kidd, *The Secret Life of Bees*

Jhumpa Lahiri, *The Namesake*

Toni Morrison, *Beloved*

Ann Patchett, *Bel Canto*

Nevil Shute, *A Town Like Alice*

Elizabeth Strout, *Olive Kitteridge*

William Styron, *Sophie's Choice*

Tom Wolfe, *The Bonfire of the Vanities*

David Wroblewski, *The Story of Edgar Sawtelle*

Markus Zusak, *The Book Thief*

JULY: SUMMER MYSTERIES

Kate Atkinson, *Case Histories*

Agatha Christie, *And Then There Were None*

Daphne du Maurier, *Rebecca*

Ken Follett, *Eye of the Needle*

Tana French, *In the Woods*

Sue Grafton, *A Is for Alibi*

Dashiell Hammett, *The Maltese Falcon*

Thomas Harris, *Red Dragon*

Louise Penny, *Still Life*

Alice Sebold, *The Lovely Bones*

Donna Tartt, *The Goldfinch*

AUGUST: CLOUD DRIFTING

John Berendt, *Midnight in the Garden of Good and Evil*

John Cheever, *The Stories of John Cheever*

Fannie Flagg, *Fried Green Tomatoes at the Whistle Stop Cafe*

Julia Glass, *Three Junes*

Arthur Golden, *Memoirs of a Geisha*

Laura Hillenbrand, *Seabiscuit*

John Irving, *A Prayer for Owen Meany*

Colleen McCullough, *The Thorn Birds*

Larry McMurtry, *Lonesome Dove*

Helen Simonson, *Major Pettigrew's Last Stand*

Virginia Woolf, *To the Lighthouse*

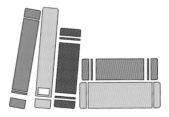

SEPTEMBER: TIME TRAVEL

Geraldine Brooks, *March*

Anthony Doerr, *All the Light We Cannot See*

Jeff Foltz, *Two Men Ten Suns*

Ben Fountain, *Billy Lynn's Long Halftime Walk*

Charles Frazier, *Cold Mountain*

David Guterson, *Snow Falling on Cedars*

Hilary Mantel, *Wolf Hall*

Boris Pasternak, *Doctor Zhivago*

Lisa See, *Snow Flower and the Secret Fan*

Kathryn Stockett, *The Help*

Alice Walker, *The Color Purple*

Baron Wormser, *Teach Us That Peace*

OCTOBER: A SHIVER IN THE AIR

A. S. Byatt, *Possession*

Charles Dickens, *The Mystery of Edwin Drood*

Gillian Flynn, *Gone Girl*

Stephen King, *Misery*

Gaston Leroux, *The Phantom of the Opera*

Carson McCullers, *Reflections in a Golden Eye*

Toni Morrison, *Beloved*

Edgar Allan Poe, *Edgar Allan Poe: The Complete Tales and Poems*

Anne Rice, *Interview with the Vampire*

Mary Shelley, *Frankenstein*

Robert Louis Stevenson, *The Strange Case of Dr. Jekyll and Mr. Hyde*

Donna Tartt, *The Little Friend*

Sarah Waters, *The Little Stranger*

H. G. Wells, *The Island of Dr. Moreau*

NOVEMBER: THE LITERATURE OF FOOD

Diana Abu-Jaber, *The Language of Baklava*

Erica Bauermeister, *The School of Essential Ingredients*

Frank Bruni, *Born Round: A Story of Family, Food, and a Ferocious Appetite*

Bill Buford, *Heat: An Amateur's Adventures as a Kitchen Slave*

Julia Child with Alex Prud'homme, *My Life in France*

Laurie Colwin, *Home Cooking* and *More Home Cooking*

M. F. K. Fisher, *The Gastronomical Me, How to Cook a Wolf, As They Were, A Cordiall Water,* and others

Daniel Halpern, *Not for Bread Alone: Writers on Food, Wine, and the Art of Eating*

Gabrielle Hamilton, *Blood, Bones & Butter*

Madhur Jaffrey, *Climbing the Mango Trees: A Memoir of a Childhood in India*

Judith Jones, *The Tenth Muse: My Life in Food*

Nicole Mones, *The Last Chinese Chef*

Molly O'Neill, *One Big Table*

Julia Reed, *Ham Biscuits, Hostess Gowns, and Other Southern Specialties: An Entertaining Life (with Recipes)*

Ruth Reichl, *Tender at the Bone, Comfort Me with Apples,* and *Garlic and Sapphires*

Calvin Trillin, *Alice, Let's Eat*

Various Editors, *Best Food Writing* annual anthologies

DECEMBER: THE LIVES OF OTHERS

Stephen Ambrose, *Undaunted Courage: Meriwether Lewis, Thomas Jefferson, and the Opening of the American West*

Maya Angelou, *I Know Why the Caged Bird Sings*

Robert Caro, *The Power Broker: Robert Moses and the Fall of New York*

Joan Didion, *The Year of Magical Thinking*

Doris Kearns Goodwin, *Lyndon Johnson and the American Dream*

Katharine Graham, *Personal History*

Alex Haley and Malcolm X, *The Autobiography of Malcolm X: As Told to Alex Haley*